United States
Department of
Agriculture

Forest Service

Northern
Research Station

General Technical
Report NRS-17

HUBBARD
BROOK
RESEARCH
H B R F FOUNDATION

Long-term Trends from Ecosystem Research at the **Hubbard Brook Experimental Forest**

John L. Campbell
Charles T. Driscoll
Christopher Eagar
Gene E. Likens
Thomas G. Siccama
Chris E. Johnson
Timothy J. Fahey
Steven P. Hamburg
Richard T. Holmes
Amey S. Bailey
Donald C. Buso

Abstract

The Hubbard Brook Experimental Forest was established by the U.S. Forest Service in 1955 as a major center for hydrologic research in the Northeast. The Hubbard Brook Ecosystem Study originated 8 years later with the idea of using the small watershed approach to study element flux and cycling and the response of forest ecosystems to disturbance. Since that time, the research program at Hubbard Brook has expanded to include various physical, chemical and biological measurements collected by researchers from a number of cooperating institutions. Collaborative, long-term data are the keystone of the Hubbard Brook Ecosystem Study and have provided invaluable insight into how ecosystems respond to disturbances such as air pollution, climate change, forest disturbance, and forest management practices. This report highlights long-term ecological trends at Hubbard Brook, provides explanations for some of the trends, and lists references from the scientific literature for further reading.

Acknowledgments

We would like to thank Kimberley M. Driscoll of Syracuse University for compiling data and developing initial graphs used in this publication. We also thank David Sleeper of the Hubbard Brook Research Foundation for advice and encouragement. The Hubbard Brook Research Foundation provided support for the photography, design, and layout of this report, through a grant from the Northeastern Ecosystem Research Cooperative. This manuscript is a contribution of the Hubbard Brook Ecosystem Study. Hubbard Brook is part of the Long-Term Ecological Research (LTER) network, which is supported by the National Science Foundation. The Hubbard Brook Experimental Forest is operated and maintained by the U.S. Forest Service, Northern Research Station, Newtown Square, Pennsylvania.

The design of this report was done by RavenMark, Inc. of Montpelier, Vermont.
Cover photos, top two: U.S. Forest Service Archives. Bottom two: Buck Sleeper.
Photographs throughout this report are by Buck Sleeper, unless otherwise noted.

The Authors

JOHN L.CAMPBELL and CHRISTOPHER EAGAR are research ecologists and AMEY S. BAILEY is a forest technician with the Northern Research Station, Durham, NH. CHARLES T. DRISCOLL is a university professor of environmental systems engineering and CHRIS E. JOHNSON is an associate professor of civil and environmental engineering, Syracuse University, Syracuse, NY. GENE E. LIKENS is an ecologist and distinguished senior scientist of the Institute of Ecosystem Studies, Millbrook, NY. THOMAS G. SICCAMA is a professor emeritus of forest ecology, Yale School of Forestry and Environmental Studies, New Haven, CT. TIMOTHY J. FAHEY is a professor of natural resources, Cornell University, Ithaca, NY. STEVEN P. HAMBURG is Director of the Global Environment Program at the Watson Institute for International Studies, Brown University, Providence, RI. RICHARD T. HOLMES is a professor emeritus of biology, Dartmouth College, Hanover, NH. DONALD C. BUSO is a biologist and manager of field research at the Hubbard Brook Experimental Forest, for the Institute of Ecosystem Studies, Millbrook, NY.

CONTENTS

Long-term Trends from
Ecosystem Research at the
**Hubbard Brook
Experimental Forest**

HUBBARD BROOK EXPERIMENTAL FOREST

The Hubbard Brook Experimental Forest (HBEF) was established in 1955 as a site of hydrologic research in New England. The site is located within the White Mountain National Forest in central New Hampshire. The emphasis of early studies at the HBEF was the impact of forest management on water yield and quality, and flood control. The Northern Research Station of the U.S. Forest Service manages the site for long-term ecosystem research and operates an on-site field station, the Robert S. Pierce Ecosystem Laboratory.

The northern hardwood forest of the HBEF is representative of much of the Northern Forest region, which covers more than 10.5 million hectares stretching from the northern woods of Maine to the Adirondack Mountains and Tug Hill regions of New York. The Northern Forest is the largest contiguous block of forest land in the eastern United States and includes a mixture of mountain ranges, rivers, lakes, and wetlands inhabited by many wildlife species (e.g., moose, pine marten, Canada lynx, song birds, peregrine falcons, common loons, bald eagles). The key issues facing the sustainable management of the Northern Forest include the impacts of forest management, land development, air pollution, climate change, introduced species, timber and fiber production, water supply and quality, and management of carbon stocks.

The Hubbard Brook Ecosystem Study (HBES) originated with the idea of using the small watershed approach to study element flux and cycling. A joint research program between the U.S. Forest Service and Dartmouth College was established by a cooperative agreement in 1963. In 1988 the HBEF was designated a Long Term Ecological Research (LTER) site by the National Science Foundation. Ongoing cooperative efforts among diverse educational and research institutions and government agencies have resulted in one of the longest and most extensive continuous databases on the hydrology, biology, geology, and chemistry of natural ecosystems. Today, more than 40 scientists from about 20 institutions participate in the HBES.

The primary goals of the HBES are: 1) to advance scientific understanding of forest and aquatic ecosystems, and their response to natural and human-induced disturbances; 2) provide scientific information required for making sound management and policy decisions; 3) to offer educational and research opportunities to students; and 4) to promote greater public awareness of ecosystem science, with a focus on the northern hardwood forest.

SITE DESCRIPTION AND CHARACTERISTICS

The HBEF is a 3,160-ha, bowl-shaped valley with hilly terrain, ranging from 222 to 1,015 m altitude; the Forest is located in the towns of Woodstock and Ellsworth, NH. The HBEF has a network of precipitation and stream-gaging stations, weather instrumentation, as well as soil and vegetation monitoring sites on small first order watersheds. There are nine first-order gaged watersheds at the HBEF, including several used for long-term experiments. Watersheds are numbered (Fig. 1) and throughout this report are referred to in the shorthand: W1, W2, etc.

The northern hardwood forest of the HBEF is representative of much of the Northern Forest region, which covers more than 10.5 million hectares stretching from the northern woods of Maine to the Adirondack Mountains and Tug Hill regions of New York.

1

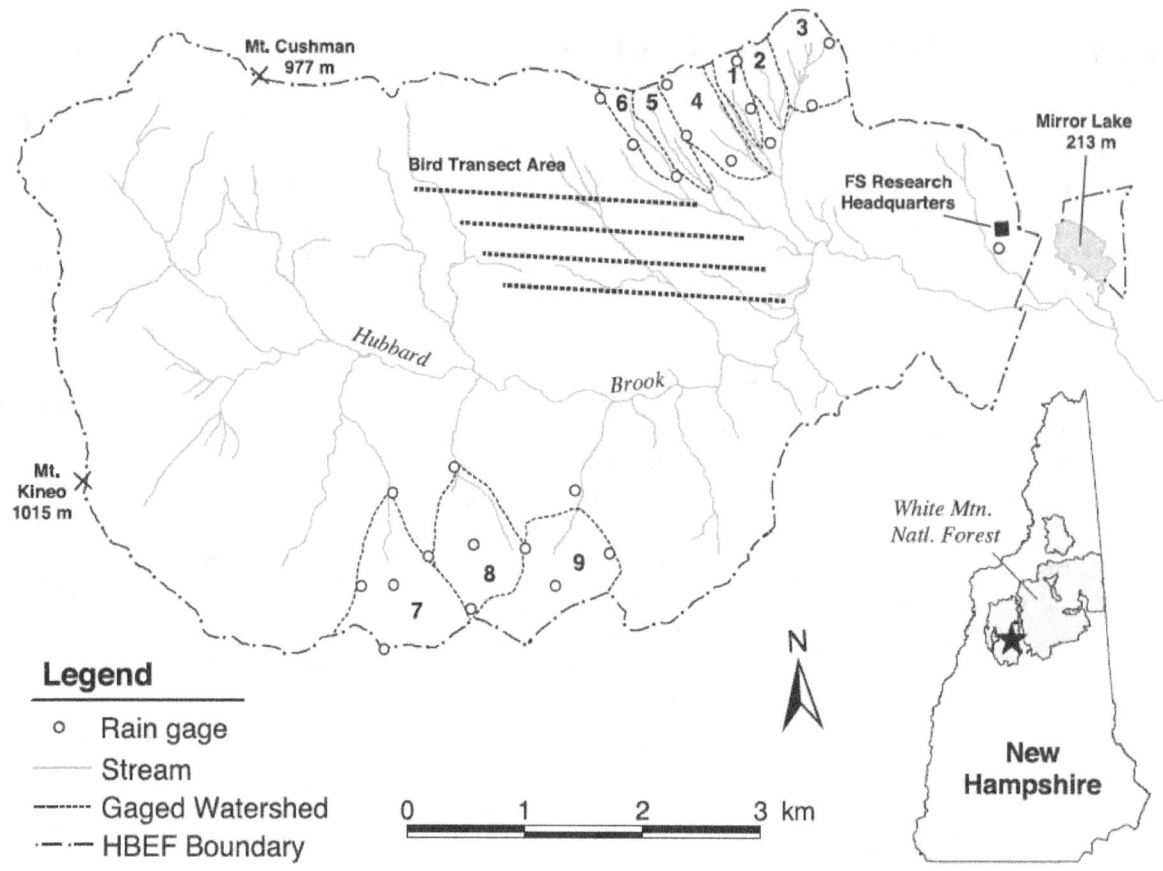

Figure 1. Site map of the Hubbard Brook Experimental Forest in the White Mountain National Forest, New Hampshire. Shown are the network of rain gages, experimental watersheds, and Mirror Lake.

Average annual precipitation is about 1,400 mm, with one-third to one-quarter as snow. Approximately 111 separate precipitation events occur each year. A snowpack usually persists from late-December until mid-April, with a peak depth in March. January averages about –9 °C, and long periods of low temperatures are common. The average July temperature is 18 °C. The average number of days without killing frost is 145; however, the growing season for trees is considered to be from 15 May to 15 September. The estimated annual evapotranspiration is about 500 mm.

Soils at the HBEF are predominantly well drained Spodosols, Typic Haplorthods, derived from glacial basal till, with sandy loam textures. These soils are acidic (pH about 4.5 or less) and relatively infertile (base saturation of mineral soil ~ 10 percent). A 20- to 200-mm thick forest floor layer is present, except where the soil surface has been disturbed by fallen trees. Soil depths, including unweathered till, are highly variable but average about 2.0 m. Soil on the ridgetops may consist of a thin accumulation of organic matter resting directly on bedrock. The separation between the pedogenic zone and unweathered till and bedrock below is indistinct. Average depth to the C horizon is about 0.6 m. At various places in the HBEF, the C horizon exists as an impermeable pan. The unsorted till includes coarse fragments (rocks) of all sizes scattered throughout the soil profile, though with increasing density with depth. In many locations, surficial boulders are prominent.

The HBEF is entirely forested, mainly with deciduous northern hardwoods: sugar maple (*Acer saccharum*), beech (*Fagus grandifolia*), and yellow birch (*Betula alleghaniensis*), and some white ash (*Fraxinus americana*) on the lower and middle slopes. Other less abundant species include mountain maple (*Acer spicatum*), striped maple (*Acer pensylvanicum*), and trembling aspen (*Populus tremuloides*). Red spruce (*Picea rubens*), balsam fir (*Abies balsamea*), and mountain paper birch (*Betula papyrifera var. cordifolia*) are abundant at higher elevations and on rock outcrops. Hemlock (*Tsuga canadensis*) is found along the main Hubbard Brook. Pin cherry (*Prunus pensylvanica*), a shade intolerant species, dominates all sites for the first decade following a major forest disturbance. The presettlement forest was dominated by red spruce, beech and birch. Logging operations began in the 1880s with major removals in the 1910s when the remaining spruce and large portions of the better quality hardwoods were removed. The 1938 hurricane and subsequent salvage logging resulted in additional tree removal and understory release. The present second-growth forest is uneven aged and comprised of about 80 to 90 percent hardwoods and 10 to 20 percent conifers.

Bluebead lily (*Clintonia borealis*) fruit

RESEARCH FOCUS

The small watershed ecosystem approach to research on nutrient cycling was pioneered at the HBEF. This approach uses the forest as a single integrated landscape unit with which scientists can conduct experiments on a watershed level, monitoring long-term changes in streamflow, nutrient cycling, forest growth, and composition. Experimental manipulations have been used extensively at the HBEF. Many whole watershed, stream, and lake manipulations have been conducted to test hypotheses, obtain quantitative information on the impacts of management options, and to validate process-based ecosystem models. Whole ecosystem manipulations conducted at the HBEF include experiments to examine forest management practices, (clearcutting, strip cutting, whole tree harvesting), the role of biological uptake on nutrient cycles (herbicide application for 3 years) and mitigation of air pollution (addition of calcium silicate).

Scientists track climatic conditions and chemical inputs through the air, rain, and snow. Researchers use long-term measurements, long-term experiments, models, and cross-site studies to investigate the effects of these conditions and how the ecosystem responds to changes in these conditions. These data are used to document and assess the ecological effects of regional and global environmental disturbances. At Hubbard Brook there are major research themes that encompass much of the ongoing research at the site, including perturbations from air pollution (such as acid rain and mercury), and the response and recovery from catastrophic (such as clearcutting) and noncatastrophic forest perturbations (such as ice storms, forest disease).

A strength of the HBES is the long-term monitoring program, which has demonstrated that short-term observations are often misleading and that decades may be required to detect real changes in complex ecosystems. The long-term record at the HBEF provides: 1) insight into ecosystem function; 2) empirical data for testing models and generating hypotheses; 3) a record of extreme or unusual events; and 4) information that is relevant to regional, national, and global issues.

Table 1. Current long-term monitoring data sets developed through the Hubbard Brook Ecosystem Study. The institution responsible for the data and initial year of data collection is indicated.

Measurement	Institution	Year
Hydrometeorological Monitoring		
Instantaneous streamflow (9 stations)	U.S. Forest Service	1956
Daily streamflow (9 stations)	U.S. Forest Service	1956
Daily precipitation (25 stations)	U.S. Forest Service	1956
Air temperature: mean, min, max (8 stations)	U.S. Forest Service	1955
Solar radiation	U.S. Forest Service	1958
Wind speed and direction	U.S. Forest Service	1965
Vapor pressure	U.S. Forest Service	1966
Weekly snow depth and snow water equivalent	U.S. Forest Service	1959
Hourly canopy surface wetness	Inst. of Ecosystem Studies	1989
Mirror Lake precipitation (2 stations)	Inst. of Ecosystem Studies	1974
Mirror Lake groundwater	Inst. of Ecosystem Studies	1978
Mirror Lake streamflow (outlet and 3 inlets)	Inst. of Ecosystem Studies	1978
Mirror Lake thermal profiles	Inst. of Ecosystem Studies	1967
Mirror Lake ice in/out dates	Inst. of Ecosystem Studies	1967
Solution and Air Chemistry		
Weekly bulk precipitation (6-10 stations)	Inst. of Ecosystem Studies	1963
Monthly soil solution chemistry within W1 and W6	Syracuse University	1984
Weekly stream chemistry at weirs of W1-9	Inst. of Ecosystem Studies	1963
Monthly stream chemistry within W1 and W6	Syracuse University	1982
Mirror Lake water column chemistry	Inst. of Ecosystem Studies	1967
Mirror Lake precipitation chemistry (2 stations)	Inst. of Ecosystem Studies	1974
Mirror Lake groundwater chemistry	Inst. of Ecosystem Studies	1980
Mirror Lake inlets/outlet chemistry (outlet and 3 inlets)	Inst. of Ecosystem Studies	1967
Air chemistry (sulfur dioxide, nitric acid, particulates, ozone)	Inst. of Ecosystem Studies	1988
Organisms		
Bird populations	Dartmouth College	1969
Phytophagous insect populations	Dartmouth College	1969
Salamander populations	Inst. of Ecosystem Studies	1970
Snail populations	Brown University	1996
Small mammals	Dartmouth and Wellesley	1986
W2 Vegetation, biomass, chemistry	University of Wyoming	1970
W4 Vegetation, biomass	U.S. Forest Service	1970
W5 Vegetation, biomass, chemistry	Cornell/Yale University	1985
W6 Vegetation, biomass, chemistry	Yale University	1965
Valley-wide vegetation	Cornell University	1997
Vegetation structure and composition (Bird Transect Area)	Dartmouth and Wellesley	1970
Fine-root, biomass, chemistry	Cornell University	1992
Microbial biomass and activity	Inst. of Ecosystem Studies	1992
Litter-Fall	Cornell University	1988
Phenology	U.S. Forest Service	1989
Soils		
Forest floor mass, chemistry (W1, W5, and W6)	Yale/Brown University	1968
Chemical and physical properties from soil pits (W5, valley-wide)	Syracuse/Cornell/ Brown University	1984
Sediment yield in weir basin	U.S. Forest Service	1956
Soil frost	U.S. Forest Service	1956
Soil temperature and moisture	U.S. Forest Service	1959

REPORT OVERVIEW

In this report, we highlight some results of long-term measurements and experiments conducted at the HBEF. The figures included show some of the more interesting long-term trends; however not all of the long-term Hubbard Brook data are presented. A complete list of long-term measurements is provided in Table 1. This report includes graphs, a description of the data and trends, the principal investigator(s) and related references. The figures are grouped into four major categories: 1) biological measurements; 2) physical measurements; 3) chemical measurements; and 4) experimental manipulations. The report targets a broad audience, including land managers, environmental protection agencies and organizations, educators and students, research scientists, and the general public.

BIOLOGICAL MEASUREMENTS

Bird abundance

Bird censuses are conducted annually between late May and early July on a 10-ha plot west of W6. The census methods, which have been used consistently since the inception of the study, consist of timed censuses along transects, mist net capture, and

Black-throated blue warbler (*Dendroica caerulescens*). Photograph by Nicholas Rodenhouse

systematic observations on individual birds. Results from this study show that the abundance of birds has declined from more than 200 individuals per 10 ha in the early 1970s to 70 to 100 per 10 ha from the early 1990s to the present. Shifts in the

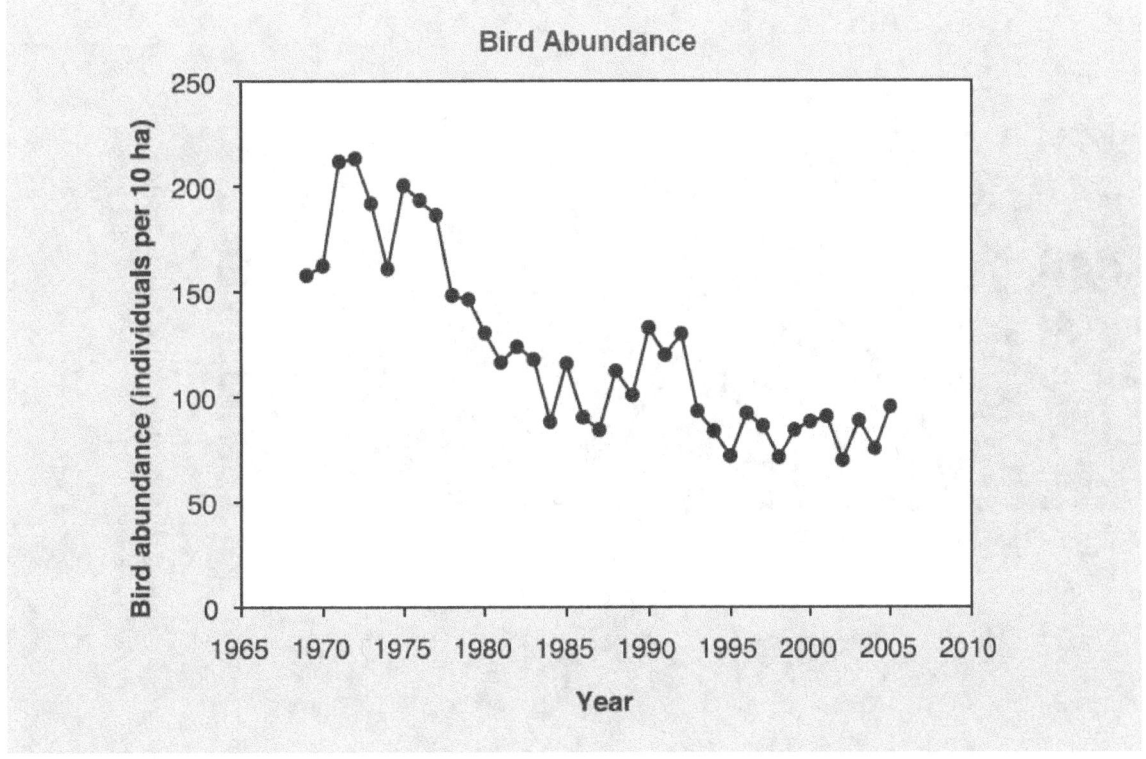

Figure 2. Number of adult birds (males and females, all species combined) breeding at the HBEF, 1969-2005.

composition of the bird community that have occurred since sampling began in 1969 can be explained in part by changes in vegetation, resulting from natural forest succession and local disturbances. Other important factors that influence bird abundance are food availability and events that occur during migration and winter periods. However, long-term declines in the overall abundance of birds remain largely unexplained and may depend upon shifts at multiple levels as the ecosystem responds to compounded stresses and perturbations. Figure updated from Holmes and Sherry (2001).

Principal Investigator:
Richard T. Holmes, Dartmouth College

Online Access:
Bird abundances – http://www.hubbardbrook.org/data/dataset.php?id=81

Associated Databases:
Lepidoptera, small mammals

Further Reading:
Holmes, R.T.; Sherry, T.W. 1988. **Assessing population trends of New Hampshire forest birds: Local versus regional patterns.** The Auk. 105: 756-768.

Holmes, R.T.; Sherry, T.W. 2001. **Thirty-year bird population abundance in an unfragmented temperate deciduous forest: Importance of habitat change.** The Auk. 118: 589-609.

Holmes, R.T.; Sherry, T.W.; Sturges, F.W. 1986. **Bird community dynamics in a temperate deciduous forest: long-term trends at Hubbard Brook.** Ecological Monographs. 56: 201-220.

Holmes, R.T.; Sturges, F.W. 1975. **Bird community dynamics and energetics in a northern hardwoods ecosystem.** Journal of Animal Ecology. 44: 175-200.

Undergraduate students updating the bird census computer database

Tree species biomass

Tree density and diameter at breast height (d.b.h.=1.37 m above ground level) have been measured at 5-year intervals on the reference watershed (W6) since 1965. Biomass is calculated using allometric equations that relate tree diameter to the mass of each species. Biomass calculations for dead trees include estimates of decay (see Siccama et al. 2007). Recent unexpected declines in total live biomass (> 10 cm d.b.h.) on W6 reflect a combination of decreased growth rates and increased mortality rates of the dominant species (sugar maple, American beech, and yellow birch). One possible explanation for the decline in sugar maple biomass is depletion of soil calcium associated with acidic deposition. While American beech biomass increased steadily from 1965 to 1997, the recent declines in the large size class (> 10 cm d.b.h.) are due primarily to beech bark

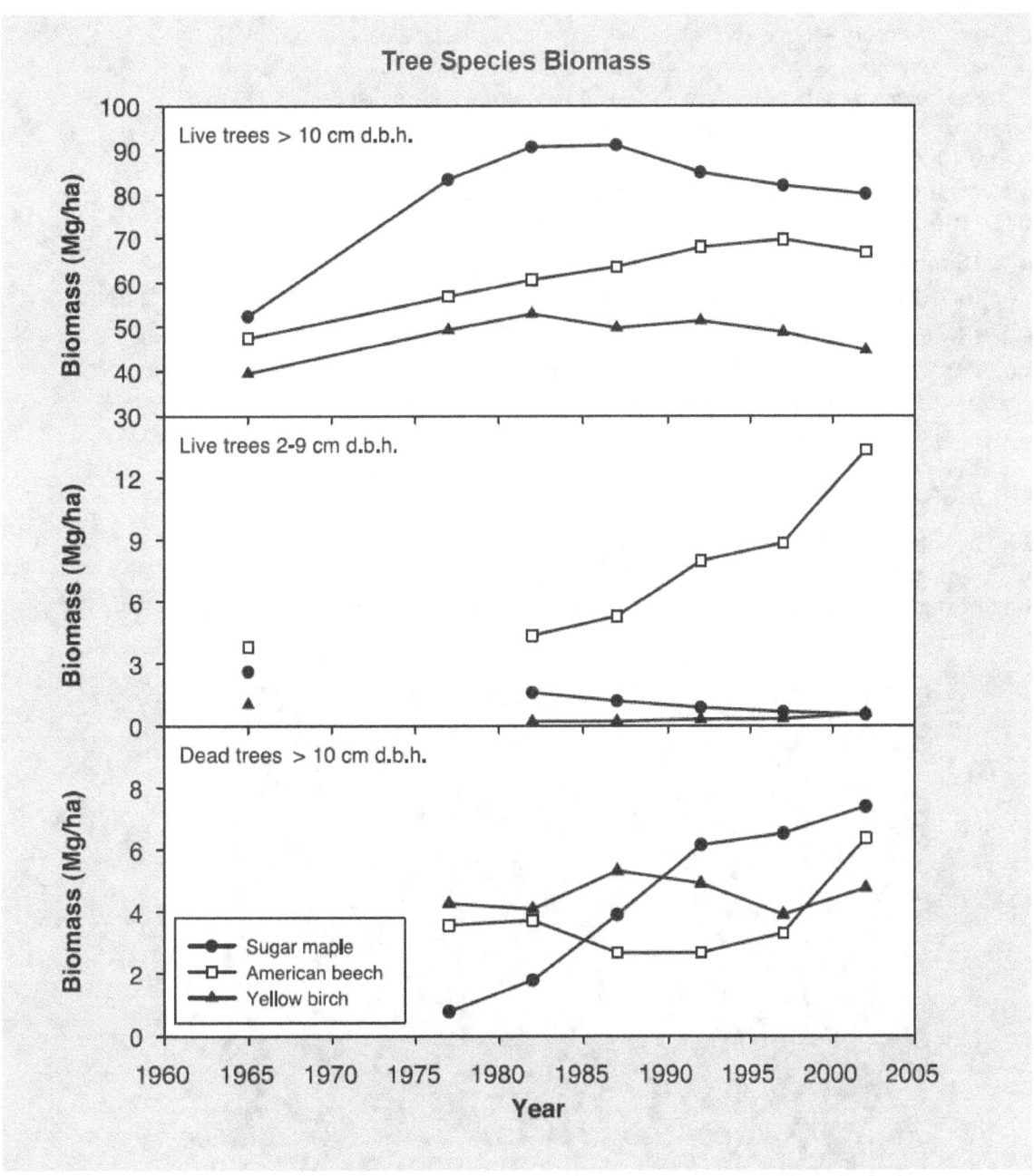

Figure 3. Tree species biomass for live and dead trees on the reference watershed W6.

disease. Beech trees affected by the disease are gradually girdled by cankers and often respond with vigorous root sprouts. Beech bark disease typically does not affect the growth of smaller trees (2 to 9 cm d.b.h.). Of the three dominant tree species, yellow birch has shown the least amount of change in biomass over the long-term record. Total live tree biomass in W6 reached a maximum earlier and at a lower level than previously predicted (see Wittaker et al. 1974), which clearly shows the importance of testing such estimates with carefully collected long-term data.

Principal Investigators:

Thomas G. Siccama, Yale University

Timothy J. Fahey, Cornell University

John J. Battles, University of California - Berkeley

Chris E. Johnson, Syracuse University

Online Access:

1965 W6 forest inventory – http://www.hubbardbrook.org/data/dataset.php?id=29

1977 W6 forest inventory – http://www.hubbardbrook.org/data/dataset.php?id=30

1982 W6 forest inventory – http://www.hubbardbrook.org/data/dataset.php?id=31

1987 W6 forest inventory – http://www.hubbardbrook.org/data/dataset.php?id=32

1992 W6 forest inventory – http://www.hubbardbrook.org/data/dataset.php?id=33

1997 W6 forest inventory – http://www.hubbardbrook.org/data/dataset.php?id=34

2002 W6 forest inventory – http://www.hubbardbrook.org/data/dataset.php?id=35

Associated Databases:

Forest inventory data (W1, W5, and Bird Transect Area)

Further Reading:

Whittaker, R.H.; Bormann, F.H.; Likens, G.E.; Siccama, T.G. 1974. **The Hubbard Brook Ecosystem Study: Forest Biomass and Production.** Ecological Monographs. 44: 233-254.

Siccama, T.G.; Denny, E. 2006. **Long-term changes in the calcium concentration of wood fern fronds [Online].** Available at http://www.hubbardbrook.org/yale/watersheds/w6/biomass-stop/how-to-quantify.htm. (accessed 12 Sept. 2006).

Siccama, T.G.; Fahey, T.J.; Johnson, C.E.; Sherry, T.; Denny, E.G.; Girdler, E.B.; Likens, G.E.; Schwarz, P. 2007. **Population and biomass dynamics of trees in a northern hardwood forest at Hubbard Brook.** Canadian Journal of Forest Research. 37: 737-749.

The northern hardwood forest at the HBEF

Tree stem counts within and between health classes

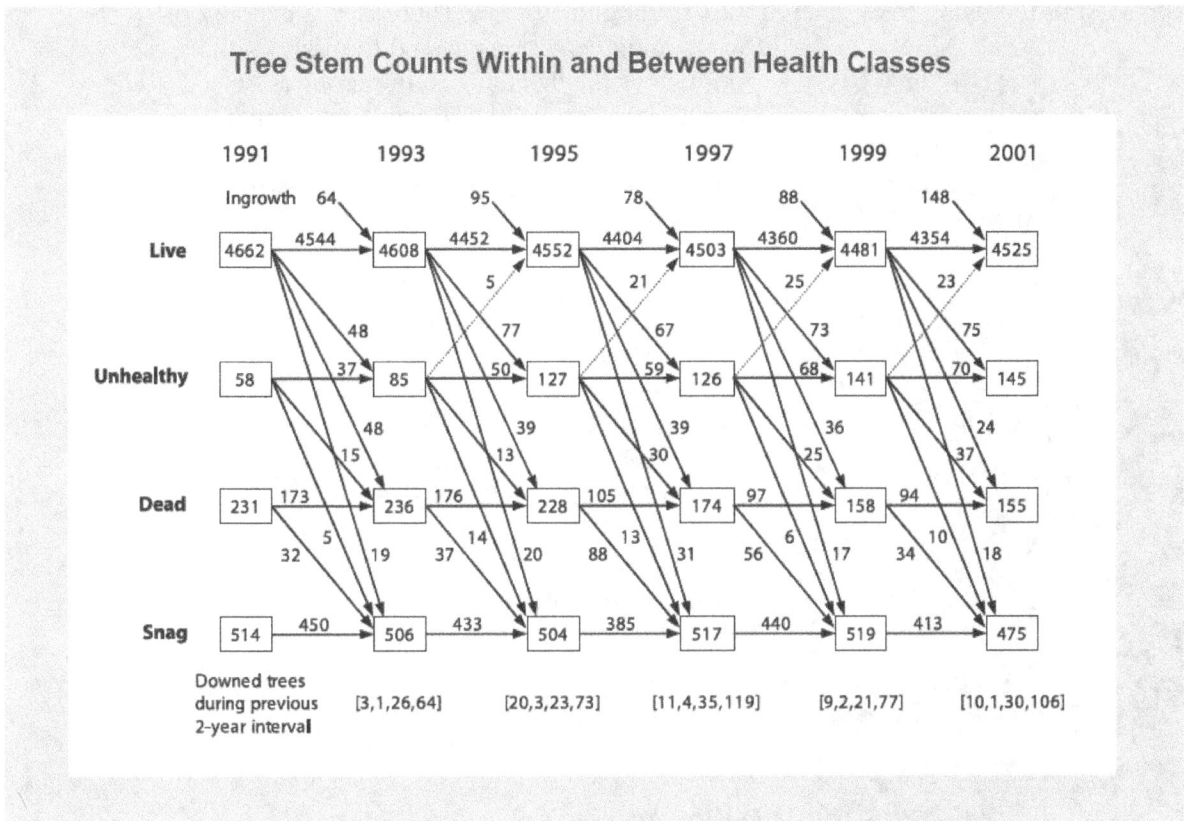

Figure 4. Tree stem counts within and between health classes at the 10-ha Bird Transect Area.

The fate of more than 5,000 trees has been tracked at the 10-ha Bird Transect Area (see Figure 2) at the HBEF as part of a continuing forest inventory that started in 1991. At the beginning of the study, all stems greater than 10-cm in the entire 10-ha area were marked with aluminum tags and the status of each tree was recorded. Trees are reassessed at 2-year intervals and these data are used to calculate the transfers of trees among five categories: 1) live and healthy; 2) unhealthy (thin crowns and few or yellowed leaves); 3) standing dead (most branches still present); 4) snag (dead trees without major branches, or broken off above breast height [1.37 m]); or 5) downed (uprooted or broken off below 1.37 m). In each 2-year resurvey, ingrowth trees, defined as those reaching the 10-cm d.b.h. threshold, are also tagged. In the diagram above, which includes 10 years of data (1991-2001), the numbers in boxes represent the number of trees in each category for each sampling year and the values associated with arrows represent the number of trees changing categories between the 2-year measurement interval. To keep the diagram

Tree tagged with identification number

legible, transfers to the downed wood category are not shown by arrows. Instead, they are given in brackets at the bottom of the figure, ordered according to the source

9

category [live (including ingrowth), unhealthy, standing dead, snag]. Of the 4720 live trees (4662 healthy and 58 unhealthy) tagged in 1991, 11 percent died over the 10-year period. Most of the dying trees entered the standing dead pool. Thereafter, a majority of the standing dead trees passed through the snag pool before finally falling to the ground. An average standing dead tree remained standing in this forest for ~7.5 years while an average snag remained standing for ~15 years. The relatively short existence of standing dead and snag trees in mature northern hardwood forests results in a low density of deteriorating trees for wildlife that use this habitat. Further calculations and summaries, including basal area, stem density, and species composition can be made using an online interactive program (see http://www.hubbardbrook.org/w6_tour/biomass-stop/phytobird.htm). Figure adapted from Siccama et al. 2007.

Principal Investigators:
Thomas G. Siccama, Yale University
Timothy J. Fahey, Cornell University
Chris E. Johnson, Syracuse University
Ellen G. Denny, Yale University and U.S. Forest Service

Online Access:
Bird Transect Area forest inventory – http://www.hubbardbrook.org/data/dataset.php?id=43

Associated Databases:
Forest inventory data (W1, W5, and W6)

Further Reading:
Siccama, T.G.; Fahey, T.J.; Johnson, C.E.; Sherry, T.; Denny, E.G.; Girdler, E.B.; Likens, G.E.; Schwarz, P. 2007. **Population and biomass dynamics of trees in a northern hardwood forest at Hubbard Brook**. Canadian Journal of Forest Research. 37:737-749.

Deteriorating trees provide habitat for wildlife

PHYSICAL MEASUREMENTS

Precipitation, stream runoff, and evapotranspiration

Precipitation and streamflow have been measured at the hydrologic reference watershed (W3) since 1957 and at eight other watersheds at the HBEF with starting dates ranging from 1956 to 1995. Precipitation is measured with rain gages located in and around each watershed, and is weighted to determine the value for the entire watershed. Streams are gaged at weirs located at the outlet of each watershed, allowing for precise measurements of streamflow. Evapotranspiration, which is a term that describes water evaporated directly from the leaves, soil or snow, is calculated by subtracting streamflow from precipitation. Variation in precipitation and streamflow is much greater than variation in evapotranspiration. Over the long-term, 61 percent of the precipitation that enters W3 leaves as streamflow, while 39 percent is returned to the atmosphere via evapotranspiration. There are no significant long-term trends in precipitation, streamflow, or evaporation although some indices suggest that the past 4 to 5 decades have been relatively wet.

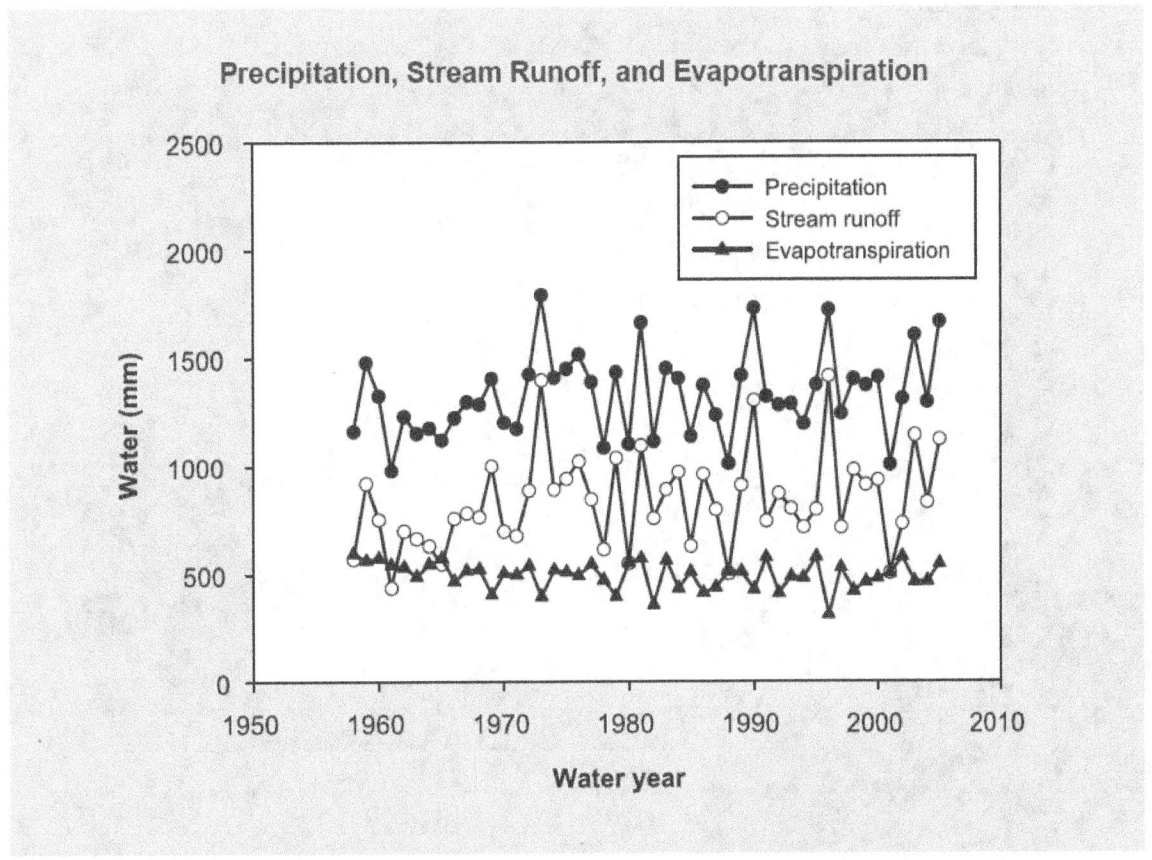

Figure 5. Precipitation, streamflow, and evapotranspiration at the hydrologic reference watershed (W3) from 1957 to 2005.

Principal Investigators:
John L. Campbell, U.S. Forest Service
Amey S. Bailey, U.S. Forest Service
Christopher Eagar, U.S. Forest Service

Online Access:
Daily precipitation by watershed – http://www.hubbardbrook.org/data/dataset.
php?id=14
Daily streamflow by watershed – http://www.hubbardbrook.org/data/dataset.php?id=2

Associated Databases:
Instantaneous streamflow, daily precipitation by rain gage

Further Reading:
Bailey, A.S.; Hornbeck, J.W.; Campbell, J.L.; Eagar, C. 2003. **Hydrometeorological database for Hubbard Brook Experimental Forest: 1955-2000.** Gen. Tech. Rep. NE-305. Newton Square, PA: U.S. Department of Agriculture, Forest Service, Northeastern Research Station. 36 p.

Measurements from stream-gaging stations are recorded and analyzed.

Photographs: (top) U.S. Forest Service Archives; (bottom) Hubbard Brook Research Foundation Archives.

Mean annual air temperature

Air temperature is measured at seven rain gage clearings (Robert S. Pierce Ecosystem Laboratory and Stations 1, 6, 14, 17, 23, and 24) located throughout the area of the experimental watersheds (see Figure 1). The oldest air temperature record dates back to 1955 at Station 1. Since that time, temperature measurements have been made consistently using hygrothermographs housed in standard shelters. Although mean annual temperature is quite variable, all locations show an upward trend, consistent with temperature records from elsewhere in the region over the same time period, as well as over a longer (>100 year) time period. Winter air temperatures at the HBEF are warming more rapidly than summer temperatures, and have greater interannual variability. In the graph above, air temperature data show significant increases (seasonal Kendall tau test, p<0.01) and give an indication of the range in air temperatures arising primarily from differences in elevation and aspect. A more thorough understanding of long-term temperature trends at the HBEF is crucial to predicting how ecosystem processes will respond to future climate change.

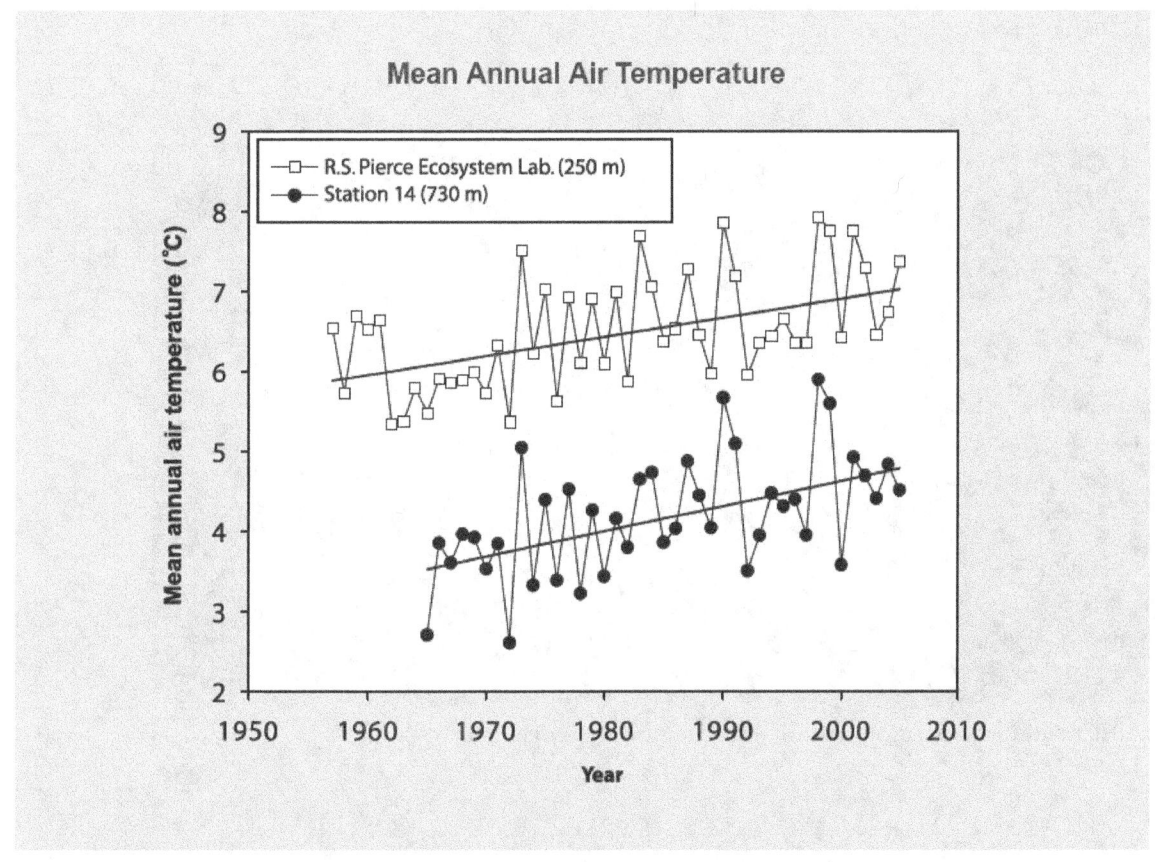

Figure 6. Mean annual air temperature at the Robert S. Pierce Ecosystem Laboratory and Station 14.

Principal Investigators:
John L. Campbell, U.S. Forest Service
Amey S. Bailey, U.S. Forest Service
Christopher Eagar, U.S. Forest Service

Online Access:
Air temperature – http://www.hubbardbrook.org/data/dataset.php?id=58

Associated Databases:
Solar radiation, soil temperature

Further Reading:
Bailey, A.S.; Hornbeck, J.W.; Campbell, J.L.; Eagar, C. 2003. **Hydrometeorological database for Hubbard Brook Experimental Forest: 1955-2000.** Gen. Tech. Rep. NE-305. Newton Square, PA: U.S. Department of Agriculture, Forest Service, Northeastern Research Station. 36 p.

View of the Hubbard Brook Valley during fall. Photograph by Jerry Franklin

Maximum snow depth and water content and snow cover duration

Snow measurements have been collected weekly at 21 locations at the HBEF for various time periods. Snow depth and water content are measured at "snow courses" that are located under the forest canopy adjacent to select rain gages. A "snow course" consists of a transect of 10 points spaced at 2-m intervals. Each week, snow depth is recorded at each point and a core of the snowpack is collected and weighed to determine snow water content. The following week, an undisturbed parallel transect, 2-m from the previous transect, is used. Mean annual maximum snow depth for the 50-year record at Station 2 is 726 mm and mean annual maximum snow water content is 189 mm. On average continuous snow cover lasts from December 25 to April 16, a total of 112 days. Despite high interannual variability, there have been slight, but statistically significant long-term

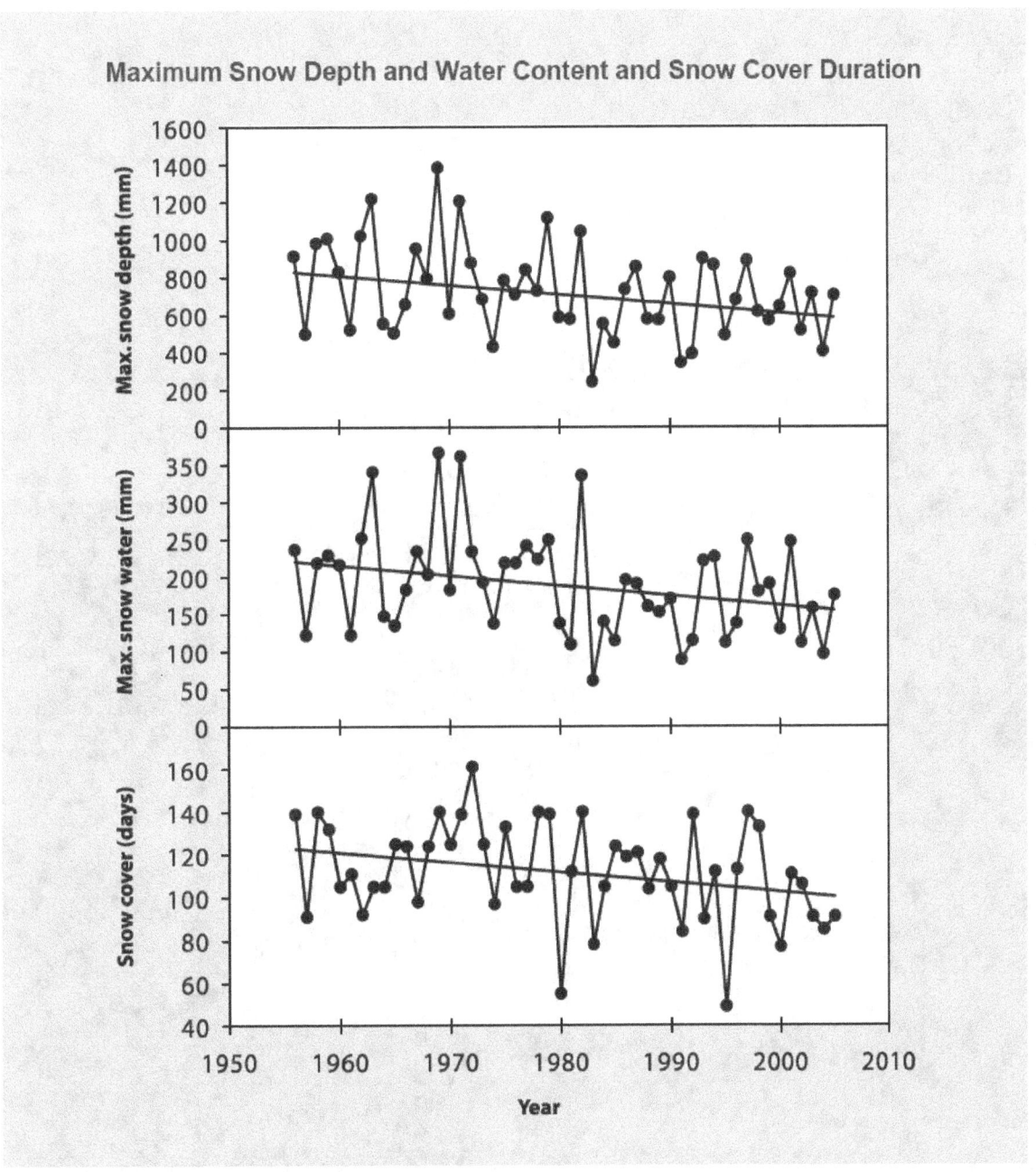

Figure 7. Maximum snow depth and water equivalence and snow cover duration at Station 2.

declines in snow depth (Mann-Kendall test, p=0.04), water content (p=0.03) and snow cover duration (p=0.04). Over the 50-year record, on average, mean annual maximum snow depth has decreased by 243 mm, snow water equivalence by 65 mm and snow cover duration by 23 days. These trends for snow are consistent with other indicators of climate change at the HBEF.

Principal Investigators:
John L. Campbell, U.S. Forest Service
Amey S. Bailey, U.S. Forest Service
Christopher Eagar, U.S. Forest Service

Online Access:
Snow depth – http://www.hubbardbrook.org/data/dataset.php?id=27
Snow water equivalence – http://www.hubbardbrook.org/data/dataset.php?id=28

Associated Databases:
Air temperature, soil frost

Further Reading:
Bailey, A.S.; Hornbeck, J.W.; Campbell, J.L.; Eagar, C. 2003. Hydrometeorological database for Hubbard Brook Experimental Forest: 1955-2000. Gen. Tech. Rep. NE-305. Newton Square, PA: U.S. Department of Agriculture, Forest Service, Northeastern Research Station. 36 p.

Snow cores are collected and weighed to measure the water content of snow. Photographs: U.S. Forest Service Archives

Days of ice cover for Mirror Lake

Mirror Lake (area, 15 ha; max. depth, 11 m) is located within the Hubbard Brook Valley and has been the subject of numerous continuous limnological investigations since the early 1960s. Routine measurements of ice cover on Mirror Lake began in 1967; however, the exact date of onset (ice in) in 1967 is uncertain so the record shown here begins in 1968. Dates for ice in and dissipation (ice out) of ice cover have been recorded using criteria that have been followed faithfully since the beginning of the study. The date of ice in is taken when more than 50 percent of the lake surface is covered with ice and remains covered. The date of ice out is taken when more than 50 percent of the lake surface is open water and the lake's surface does not refreeze. The long-term trend in ice covered days (number of days between ice in and ice out) shows an overall decline of about 0.5 days per year during the long-term record. The ice out date is in April and has been occurring significantly earlier on average, whereas there has been no significant change in the ice in date. The earlier ice out date in April with time for Mirror Lake is correlated with increased average air temperatures in April. This pattern is consistent with the pattern of global warming, but the interannual variability is large and most of the significant change occurred before 1985. Figure adapted from Likens (2000).

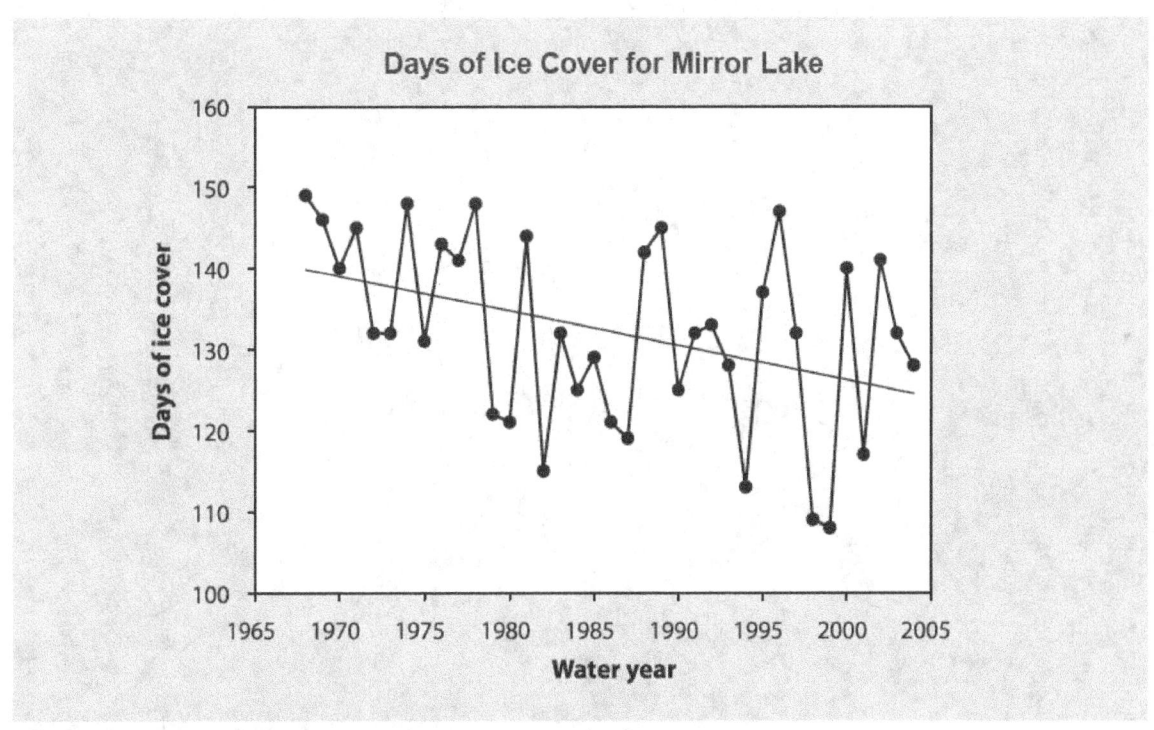

Figure 8. Days of ice cover for Mirror Lake from 1968 to 2004.

Principal Investigator:
Gene E. Likens, Institute of Ecosystem Studies

Online Access:
Mirror Lake ice cover - http://www.hubbardbrook.org/data/dataset.php?id=118

Associated Databases:
Air temperature, Mirror Lake thermal profiles

Further Reading:
Likens, G.E. 2000. **A long-term record of ice-cover for Mirror Lake, New Hampshire: Effects of global warming?** Verhandlungen Internationale Vereinigung für theoretische und angewandte Limnologie. 27: 2765-2769.

Ice out at Mirror Lake. Photograph by Donald Buso

CHEMICAL MEASUREMENTS

Chloride in Mirror Lake

The increase in chloride concentrations at the northeast inlet and Mirror Lake outlet is caused primarily by runoff of road salt used to de-ice Interstate 93 (I-93). Much of the road salt is transported to Mirror Lake via the northeast inlet stream, which provides approximately 30-50 percent of all the chloride to the lake but only a small fraction of total streamflow (2 percent). Chloride concentrations at the northeast inlet began to increase in 1970, when I-93 opened, despite the installation of an earthen diversion dam. The decrease in concentrations in 1995-96 was likely due to dilution from higher than usual precipitation. After 2000, further declines resulted from installing a plastic liner adjacent to the highway to divert contaminated runoff away from the lake. Unlike the northeast inlet, chloride concentrations at the lake outlet have continued to increase because of small increases in salt use on local roads within the west and northwest inlets to the lake, which carry 47 percent of the water inflow.

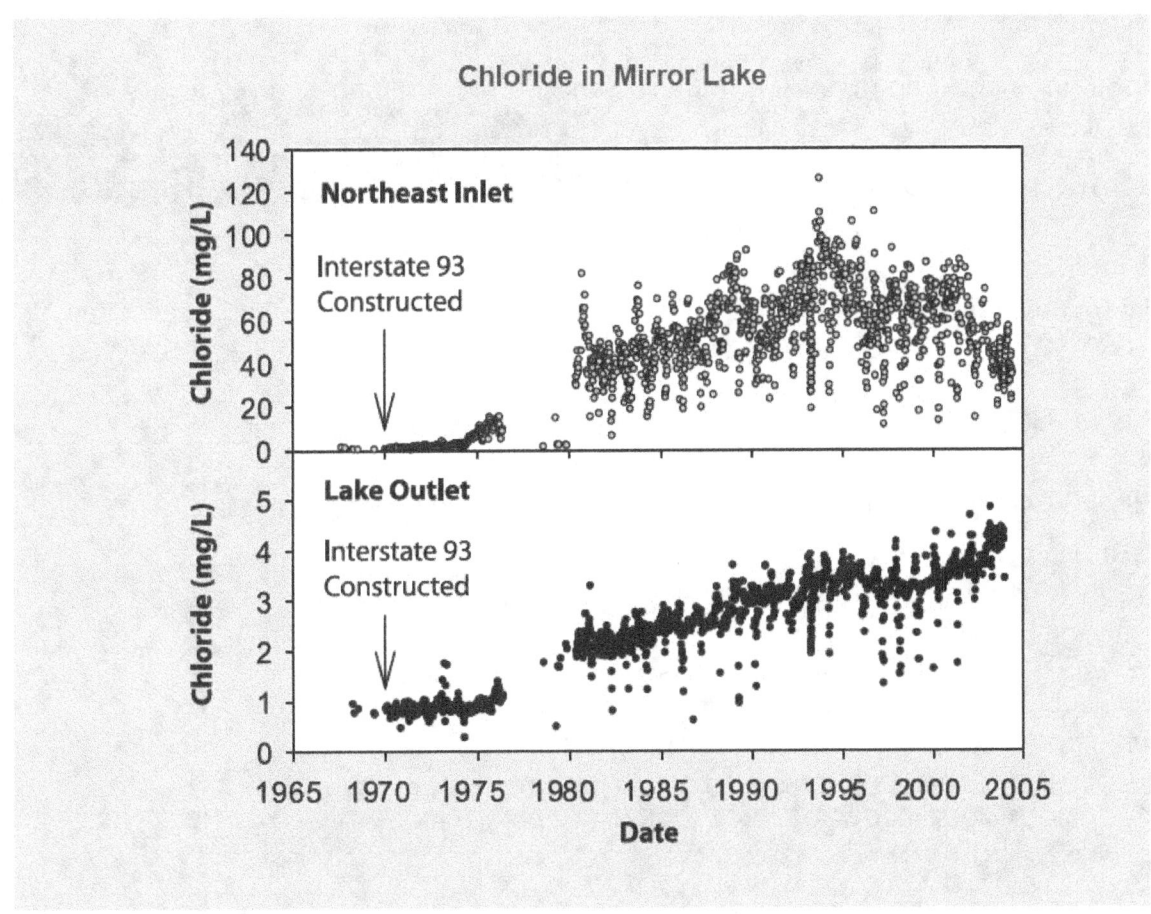

Figure 9. Chloride concentrations at the northeast inlet to Mirror Lake and at the Mirror Lake outlet.

Mirror Lake and its gaged outlet.
Photographs: (left) U.S. Forest Service Archives,
and (right) Judy Brown

Principal Investigator:
Gene E. Likens, Institute of Ecosystem Studies

Online Access:
Mirror Lake northeast inlet chemistry – http://www.hubbardbrook.org/data/dataset.php?id=87

Mirror Lake outlet chemistry – http://www.hubbardbrook.org/data/dataset.php?id=86

Associated Databases:
Chemistry of Mirror Lake water column, west inlet, northwest inlet

Further Reading:
Bormann, F.H.; Likens, G.E. 1985. **Air and watershed management and the aquatic ecosystem.** In: Likens, G.E., ed. An ecosystem approach to aquatic ecology: Mirror Lake and its environment. New York: Springer-Verlag: 436-444.

Rosenberry, D.O.; Bukaveckas, P.A.; Buso, D.C.; Likens, G.E.; Shapiro, A.M.; Winter, T.C. 1999. **Movement of road salt to a small New Hampshire lake.** Water, Air, and Soil Pollution. 109: 179-206.

Sulfur dioxide emissions versus sulfate concentrations

In the national debate about acid rain during the 1980s, there was insufficient data to show how sulfur emitted to the atmosphere from pollution sources is related to sulfur concentrations in precipitation and stream water. Since that time, there have been improvements in the methods for determining the quantity of sulfur emitted to the atmosphere and there are now longer records of weekly precipitation and stream water chemistry data at the HBEF. These factors have made it possible to show that there is a strong significant relationship between sulfur dioxide emissions from source areas in the United States and Canada and sulfate concentrations in bulk precipitation at the HBEF. Long-term data (1965-2003) from the HBEF show that reducing emissions of sulfur dioxide decreases the concentration of sulfate in bulk precipitation, ultimately reducing sulfate concentrations in stream water. Figure adapted from Likens et al. (2002).

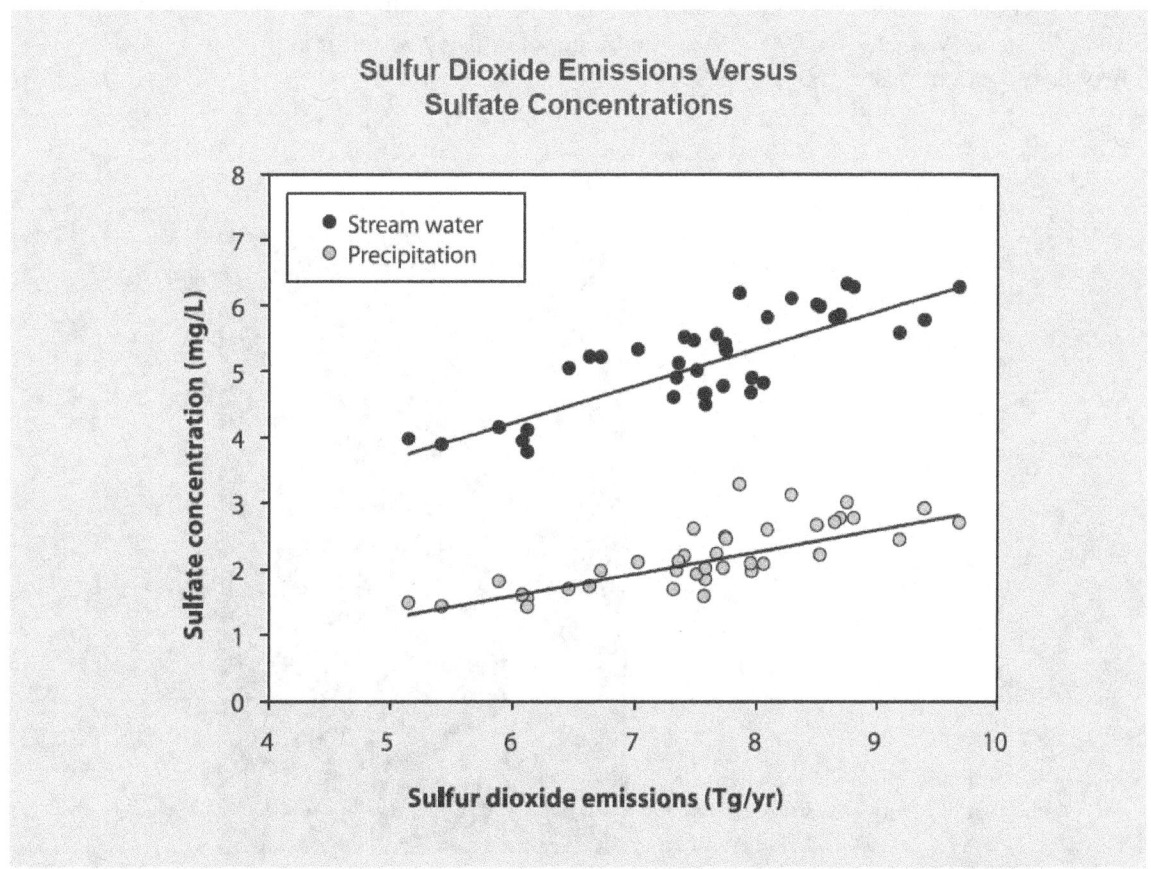

Figure 10. Sulfur dioxide emissions versus sulfate concentrations in precipitation and stream water.

Principal Investigator:

Gene E. Likens, Institute of Ecosystem Studies

Online Access:

Stream water chemistry (W6) – http://www.hubbardbrook.org/data/dataset.php?id=8
Bulk precipitation chemistry (W6) – http://www.hubbardbrook.org/data/dataset.php?id=20

Associated Databases:

Stream water chemistry (W1-5, and W7-9), Bulk precipitation chemistry (W1-5, and W7-9)

Further Reading:

Likens, G.E.; Buso, D.C.; Butler, T.J. 2005. **Long-term relationships between SO$_2$ and NO$_x$ emissions and SO$_4$$^{2-}$ and NO$_3$- concentration in bulk deposition at the Hubbard Brook Experimental Forest, New Hampshire**. Journal of Environmental Monitoring. 7: 964-968.

Likens, G.E.; Driscoll, C.T.; Buso, D.C.; Mitchell, M.J.; Lovett, G.M.; Bailey, S.W.; Siccama, T.G.; Reiners, W.A.; Alewell, C. 2002. **The biogeochemistry of sulfur at Hubbard Brook**. Biogeochemistry. 60: 235-316.

Sampling precipitation chemistry.
Photograph: Hubbard Brook Research
Foundation Archives

Stream water concentrations of base cations, sulfate and nitrate, and pH

Stream water chemistry has been monitored at the outlet of the biogeochemical reference watershed (W6) since 1963. Declines in stream water sulfate during this time have coincided with decreases in atmospheric deposition of sulfur. During the last 35 years, nitrate concentrations have also declined in stream water. However, the trend in stream water nitrate has not been clearly linked to atmospheric nitrogen deposition, and the cause of the trend is not yet well established. The recent trend of decreasing nitrate in W6 was interrupted by two noncatastrophic disturbance events: a soil freezing event in 1989 and an ice storm in 1998. Declines in nitrate and sulfate have been balanced to some degree by declines in concentrations of base cations. The pH of stream water has increased slightly as streams recover from acidic deposition. However, recovery has been slower than anticipated because base cations have been depleted from the soil due to acidic deposition and to a lesser extent, a reduction in atmospheric inputs of base cations. Additionally, years of high sulfur deposition have caused sulfur to accumulate in the soil, which is now being released to surface waters as sulfate. The slow recovery response demonstrates the need for long-term measurements. Figure adapted from Likens et al. (1996).

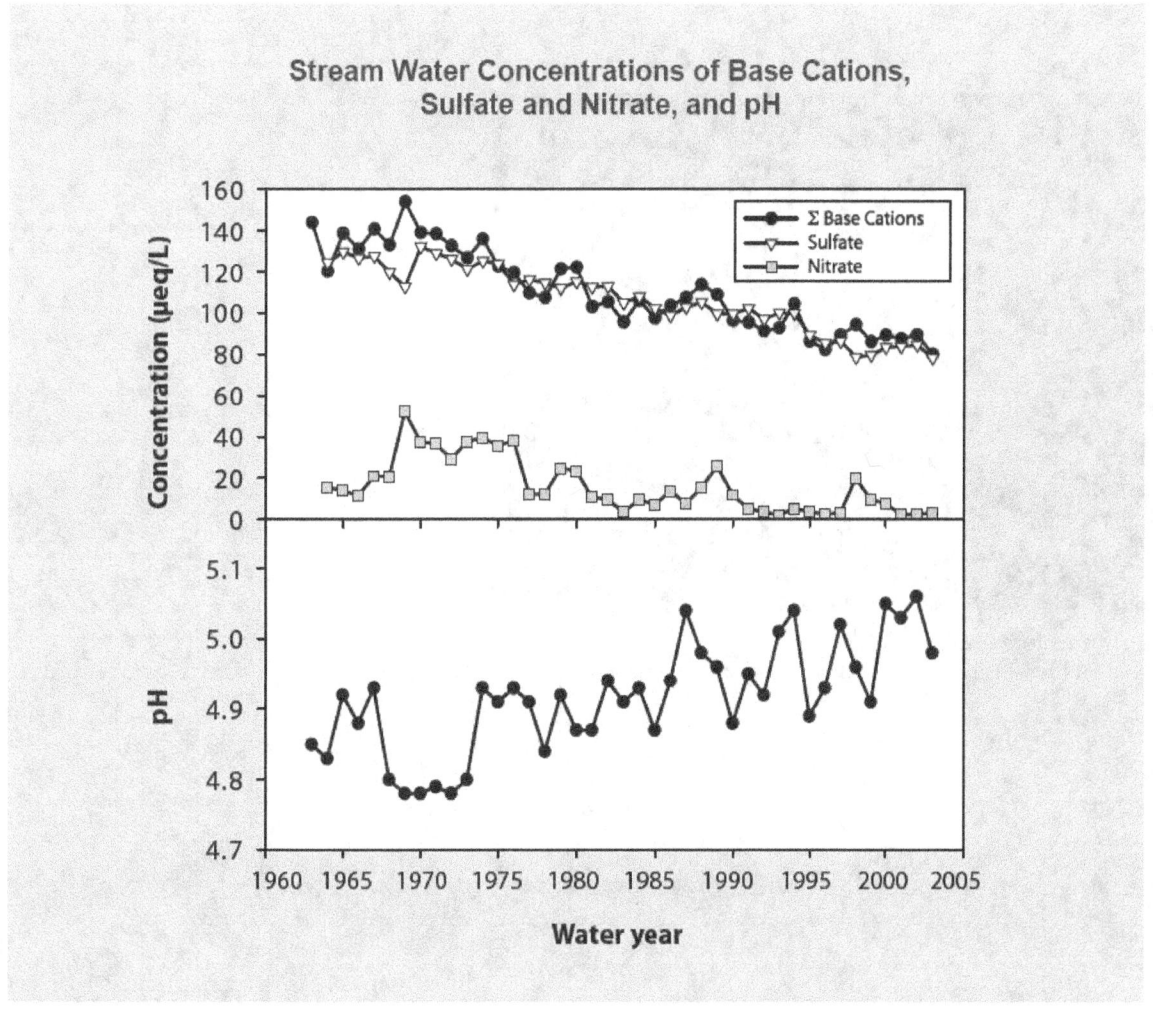

Figure 11. Stream water concentrations of base cations, sulfate and nitrate, and pH at W6.

Principal Investigator:
Gene E. Likens, Institute of Ecosystem Studies

Online Access:
Stream water chemistry (W6) – http://www.hubbardbrook.org/data/dataset.php?id=8

Associated Databases:
Stream water chemistry (W1-5, and W7-9)

Further Reading:

Likens, G.E.; Driscoll, C.T.; Buso, D.C. 1996. **Long-term effects of acid rain: response and recovery of a forest ecosystem. Science.** 272: 244-246.

Likens, G.E.; Driscoll, C.T.; Buso, D.C.; Mitchell, M.J.; Lovett, G.M.; Bailey, S.W.; Siccama, T.G.; Reiners, W.A.; Alewell, C. 2002. **The biogeochemistry of sulfur at Hubbard Brook. Biogeochemistry.** 60: 235-316.

Likens, G.E.; Driscoll, C.T.; Buso, D.C.; Siccama, T.G.; Johnson, C.E.; Lovett, G.M.; Fahey, T.J.; Reiners, W.A.; Ryan, D.F.; Martin, C.W.; Bailey, S.W. 1998. **The biogeochemistry of calcium at Hubbard Brook.** Biogeochemistry. 41: 89-173.

Driscoll, C.T.; Lawrence, G.B.; Bulger, A.J.; Butler, T.J.; Cronan, C.S.; Eagar, C.; Lambert, K.F.; Likens, G.E.; Stoddard, J.L.; Weathers, K.C. 2001. **Acidic deposition in the northeastern United States: Sources and inputs, ecosystem effects, and management strategies.** BioScience. 51: 180-198.

Sampling streams for chemical analyses
Photograph: Hubbard Brook Research Foundation Archives

Concentrations of forms of aluminum in soil solutions

Shown are two forms of dissolved aluminum in soil waters: total dissolved aluminum and organic aluminum. The difference between total dissolved and organic aluminum represents the inorganic form of dissolved aluminum. Dissolved inorganic aluminum is considered to be toxic at high concentrations. Organic aluminum is considered to be less toxic. Figure 12 shows trends in aluminum in forest floor (Oa horizon) and lower mineral soil (Bs horizon) solutions. The mobilization of aluminum is a consequence of inputs of acidic deposition to forest soils. In soil solutions draining the upper organic horizon, aluminum is largely in the nontoxic organic form. In the mineral soil, toxic inorganic aluminum is mobilized and is ultimately transported to streams. Shown are

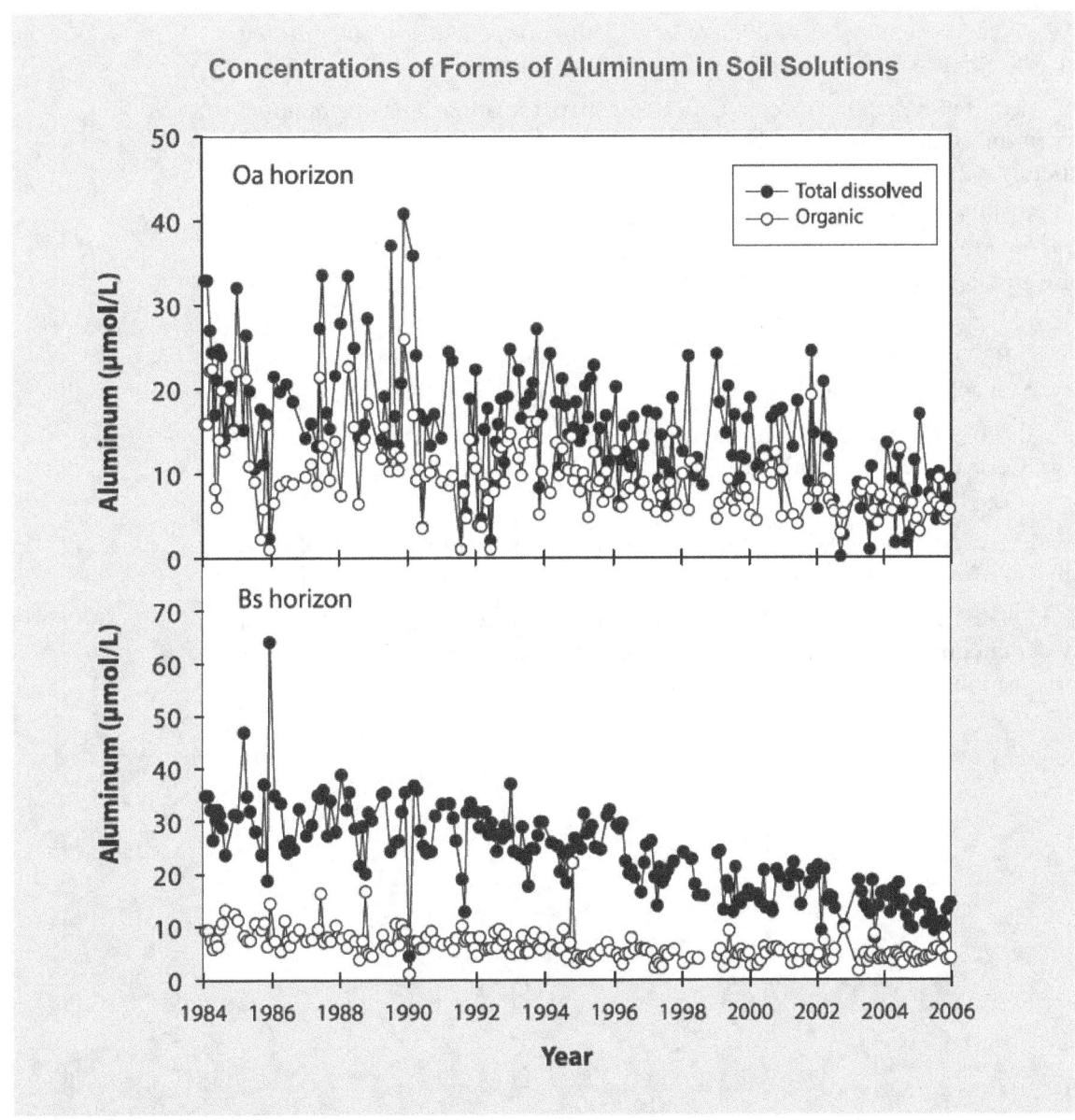

Figure 12. Concentrations of total dissolved and organic aluminum in soil solutions at the high elevation hardwood zone in W6.

soil solutions collected in the high elevation hardwood zone. This is an area of the HBEF where effects of acidic deposition on soils are greatest. Over the longterm, concentrations of both forms of aluminum have decreased, consistent with declines in inputs of acidic deposition to the HBEF.

Principal Investigator:

Charles T. Driscoll, Syracuse University

Online Access:

Soil solution chemistry (W6) – http://www.hubbardbrook.org/data/dataset.php?id=62

Associated Databases:

Precipitation and stream water chemistry (W6)

Further Reading:

Driscoll, C.T.; van Breemen, N.; Mulder, J. 1985. **Aluminum chemistry in a forested Spodosol**. Soil Science Society America Journal. 49: 437-444.

Lawrence, G.B.; Fuller, R. D.; Driscoll, C.T. 1986. **Spatial relationships of aluminum chemistry in the streams of the Hubbard Brook Experimental Forest, New Hampshire**. Biogeochemistry. 2: 115-135.

Driscoll, C.T.; Johnson, N.M.; Likens, G. E.; Feller, M.C. 1988. **The effects of acidic deposition on stream water chemistry: a comparison between Hubbard Brook, New Hampshire and Jamieson Creek, British Columbia**. Water Resources Research. 24: 195-200.

Lawrence, G.B.; Driscoll, C.T.; Fuller, R.D. 1988. **Hydrologic control of aluminum chemistry in an acidic headwater stream**. Water Resources Research. 24: 659-669.

Driscoll, C.T.; Postek, K.M. 1995. **The chemistry of aluminum in surface waters**. In: Sposito, G., ed. The Environmental Chemistry of Aluminum. Chelsea, MI: Lewis Publishers: 363-418.

Palmer, S.M.; Driscoll, C.T. 2002. **Acidic deposition. Decline in mobilization of toxic aluminum**. Nature. 417: 242-243.

Palmer, S.M.; Driscoll, C.T.; Johnson, C.E. 2004. **Long-term trends in soil solution and stream water chemistry at the Hubbard Brook Experimental Forest: relationship with landscape position**. Biogeochemistry. 68: 51-70.

Lead in precipitation, stream water, and the forest floor

In the 1970s, the sale of gasoline containing lead additives was restricted in the United States under the Clean Air Act. Since then, the amount of lead emitted to the atmosphere has declined resulting in lower concentrations of lead in precipitation and stream water. However, despite lower inputs, lead continues to accumulate in the forest ecosystem at the HBEF due to extremely low losses in drainage water. Since lead was assumed to have a long residence time in the forest floor, the declining rate of deposition was expected to simply slow the rate of accumulation. However, studies at the HBEF and elsewhere in the northeastern United States have shown significant net decreases in the amount of lead in the forest floor. Lead now appears to be accumulating in the mineral soil. It is unclear what caused the increase in forest floor lead in 1992 at the HBEF; however, it may be related to the high forest floor organic matter mass measured in samples collected that year. Based on these field observations, it is clear that lead is more mobile than previously thought, suggesting a continued threat of lead pollution in drainage water.

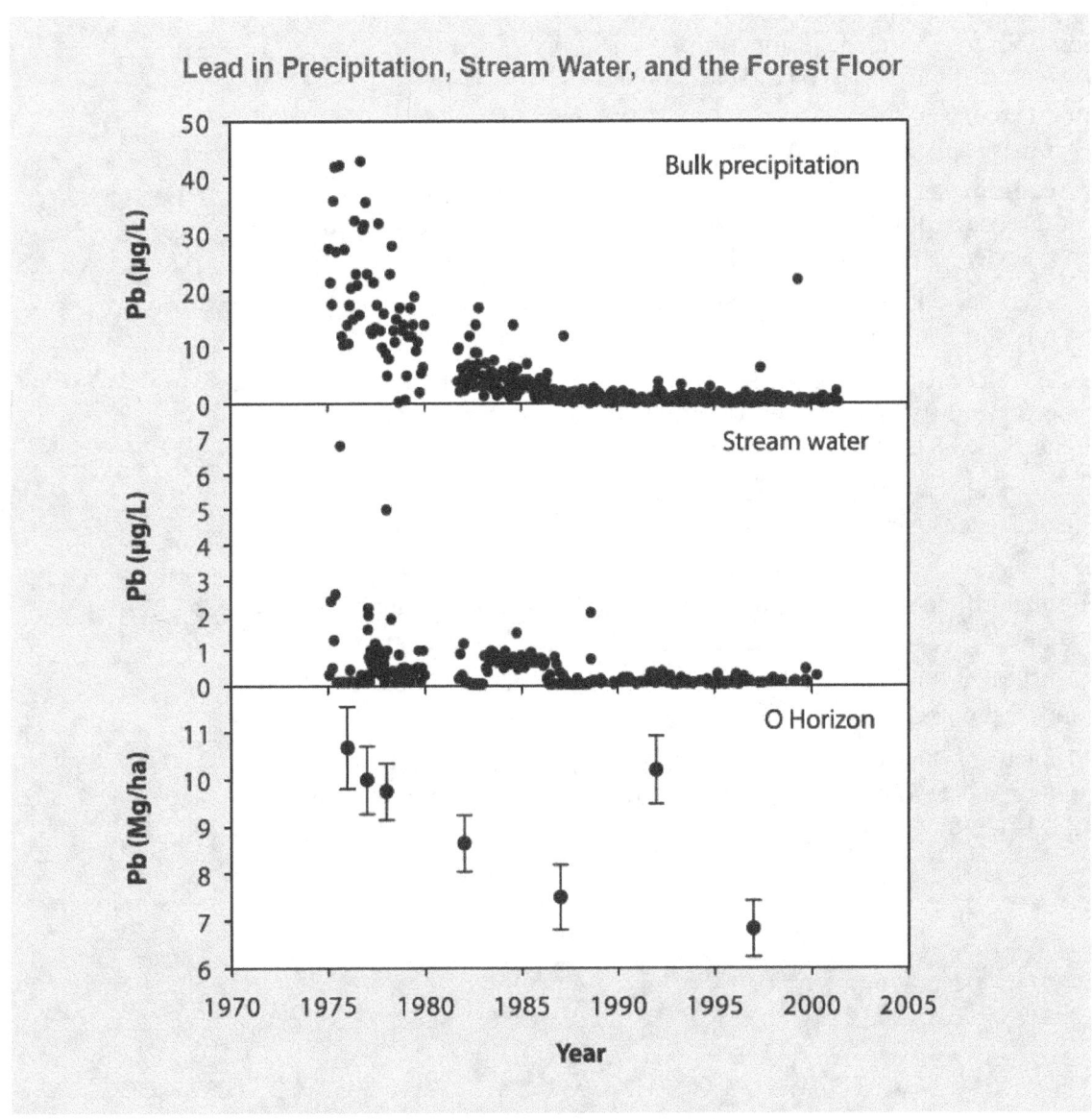

Figure 13. Lead in precipitation, stream water, and the forest floor (±SE).

Principal Investigator:

Chris E. Johnson, Syracuse University
Thomas G. Siccama, Yale University

Online Access:

1976 forest floor mass and chemistry (W6) –
http://www.hubbardbrook.org/data/dataset.php?id=69

1977 forest floor mass and chemistry (W6) –
http://www.hubbardbrook.org/data/dataset.php?id=70

1978 forest floor mass and chemistry (W6) –
http://www.hubbardbrook.org/data/dataset.php?id=71

1982 forest floor mass and chemistry (W6) –
http://www.hubbardbrook.org/data/dataset.php?id=72

1987 forest floor mass and chemistry (W6) –
http://www.hubbardbrook.org/data/dataset.php?id=73

1992 forest floor mass and chemistry (W6) –
http://www.hubbardbrook.org/data/dataset.php?id=74

1997 forest floor mass and chemistry (W6) –
http://www.hubbardbrook.org/data/dataset.php?id=75

Associated Databases:

Forest floor mass and chemistry (W1 and W5)

Further Reading:

Johnson, C.E.; Petras, R.J. 1998. **Lead and zinc fractionation in a forest Spodosol.** Soil Science Society of America Journal. 62: 782-789.

Johnson, C.E.; Petras, R.J.; April, R.H.; Siccama, T.G. 2004. **Post-glacial lead dynamics in a forest soil.** Water, Air and Soil Pollution: Focus. 4: 579-590.

Johnson, C.E.; Siccama, T.G.; Driscoll, C.T.; Likens, G.E.; Moeller, R.E. 1995. **Changes in lead biogeochemistry in response to decreasing atmospheric inputs.** Ecological Applications. 5 :813-822.

Siccama, T.G.; Smith, W.H. 1978. **Lead accumulation in a northern hardwood forest.** Environmental Science and Technology. 12: 593-594.

Smith, W.H.; Siccama, T.G. 1981. **The Hubbard Brook Ecosystem Study: biogeochemistry of lead in the northern hardwood forest.** Journal of Environmental Quality. 10: 323-333.

Wang, E.X.; Bormann, F.H.; Benoit, G. 1995. **Evidence of complete retention of atmospheric lead in the soils of northern hardwood forested ecosystems.** Environmental Science and Technology. 29: 735-739.

Yanai, R.D.; Ray, D.G.; and Siccama, T.G. 2004. **Lead reduction and redistribution in the forest floor in New Hampshire northern hardwoods.** Journal of Environmental Quality. 33: 141-148.

Forest floor carbon and nitrogen

The forest floor (Oi, Oe and Oa horizons) of W6 has been sampled and analyzed for carbon and nitrogen content seven times since 1976. All samples were collected from randomly selected grid cells in W6, and the sampling intensity steadily increased from 58 samples per year in 1976 to 100 in 2002. Samples from 1976 and 1977 were combined to make the sample size more comparable to those in later years. Over the 25 years of monitoring, there has been no significant change in either the carbon or nitrogen content of the forest floor. Linear regression analysis shows an insignificant long-term increase of 95 kg carbon per ha/yr and an increase of 1.7 kg nitrogen per ha/yr. There is a significant increase in the carbon:nitrogen ratio for the whole forest floor over 25 years, reflecting the greater increase in carbon relative to nitrogen. Though the changes in forest floor carbon and nitrogen contents are subtle, the shifting carbon:nitrogen ratio suggests that the forest floor has been dynamic over the 25 years of record. This change in the carbon:nitrogen ratio may slow organic matter decomposition if sufficient nitrogen to support microbial growth cannot be obtained from the decomposing material or soil solution. Forest floor samples are permanently stored in the sample archive at Hubbard Brook, along with many other types of samples, not only to construct longer records for monitoring, but also to apply new analytical techniques to preserved samples.

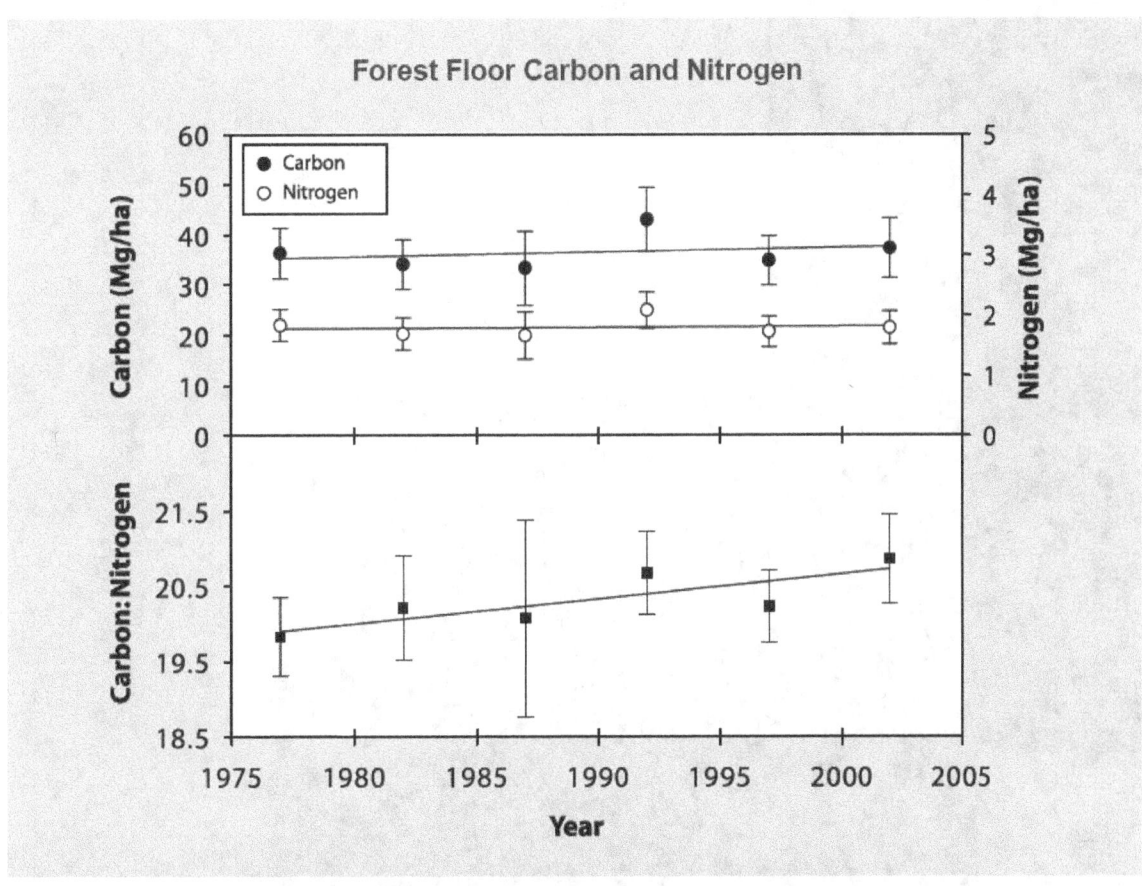

Figure 14. Forest floor carbon and nitrogen (±95 percent confidence interval) at W6.

Principal Investigator:
Steven P. Hamburg, Brown University
Thomas G. Siccama, Yale University

Associated Databases:
Forest floor mass and chemistry (W1 and W5)

Further Reading:

Huntington, T.G.; Ryan, D.F.; Hamburg, S.P. 1988. **Estimating soil nitrogen and carbon pools in a northern hardwood forest ecosystem.** Soil Science Society of America Journal. 52: 1162-1167.

Yanai, R.D.; Stehman, S.V.; Arthur, M.A.; Prescott, C.E.; Friedland, A.J.; Siccama T.G.; Binkley, D. 2003. **Detecting change in forest floor carbon.** Soil Science Society of America Journal. 67: 1583-1593.

The forest floor is the dark horizon near the surface. It is sampled with a pin block (below) which is used to extract the intact organic matter for analyses. Photographs: U.S. Forest Service Archives

EXPERIMENTAL MANIPULATIONS

Nitrate concentrations in stream water

Biologically important nutrients, such as nitrogen, are usually strongly retained in northern hardwood forest ecosystems. When northern forest ecosystems are disturbed, however, the nitrogen cycle is disrupted, resulting in high leaching losses of nitrate. This stream water nitrate response is demonstrated by comparing long-term trends of annual volume-weighted concentrations of nitrate in the reference (W6), and cut (W2 devegetation and herbicide treatment, 1965-1968; W4 strip-cut, 1970-1974; W5 clearcut, 1983-1984) watersheds. The increase in stream water nitrate after cutting generally only lasts a few years because nitrate is readily retained by regrowing vegetation. In addition to these results, there have been some unexpected patterns in long-term nitrogen retention data from these experimentally cut watersheds. During the 10 to 15 year aggrading phase of W2 and W4, inputs of nitrogen were strongly retained and nitrate leaching losses were low. In recent years, this pattern has shifted such that nitrate loss in cut watersheds exceeds values observed in the reference watershed. If this pattern remains consistent across cut watersheds, nitrate concentrations in W5 would soon exceed concentrations in the reference watershed. Without long-term studies such unexpected and interesting findings would not be discovered.

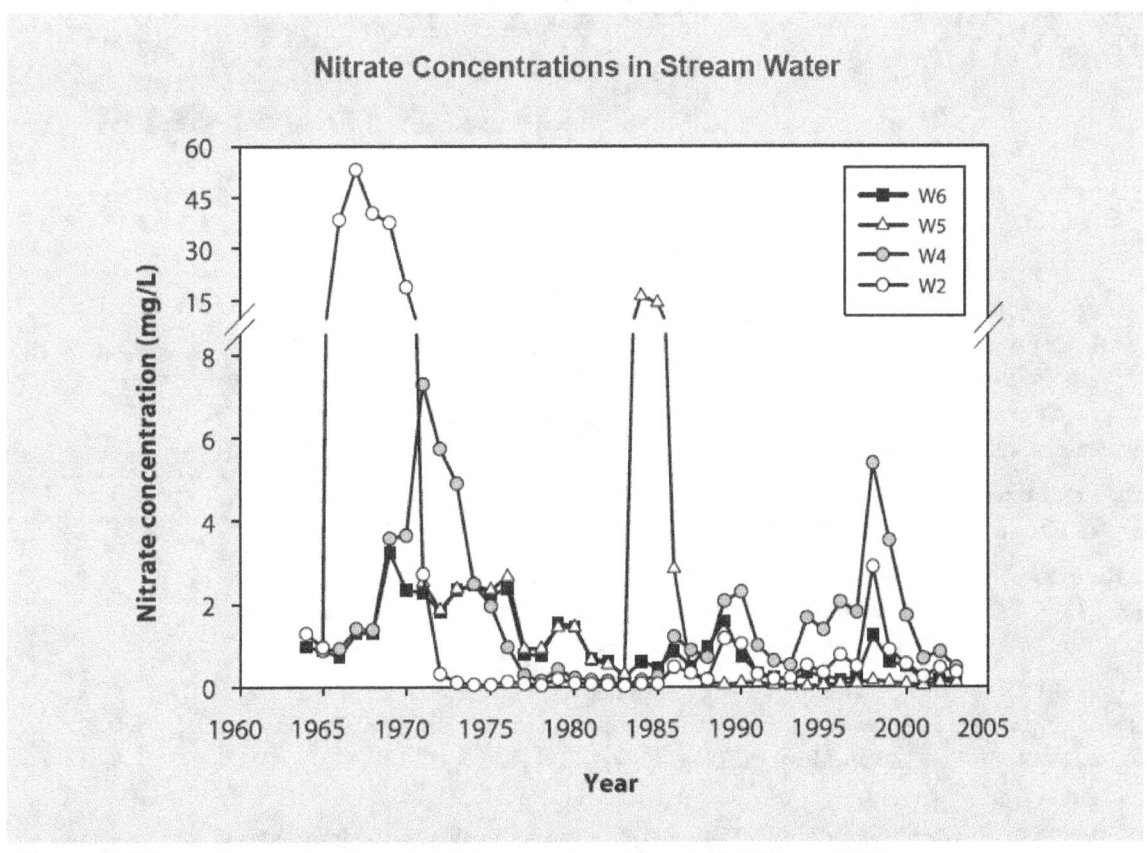

Figure 15. Nitrate concentrations in stream water at W2, W4, W5, and W6.

Stream samples are stored in the archive building at the HBEF for future analyses. Photographs: (top) U.S. Forest Service Archives, and (bottom) Buck Sleeper

Principal Investigator:
Gene E. Likens, Institute of Ecosystem Studies

Online Access:
Stream water chemistry (W2) - http://www.hubbardbrook.org/data/dataset.php?id=4
Stream water chemistry (W4) - http://www.hubbardbrook.org/data/dataset.php?id=6
Stream water chemistry (W5) - http://www.hubbardbrook.org/data/dataset.php?id=7
Stream water chemistry (W6) - http://www.hubbardbrook.org/data/dataset.php?id=8

Associated Databases:
Stream water chemistry (W1, W3 and W7-9)

Further Reading:
Bormann, F.H.; Likens, G.E.; Fisher, D.W.; Pierce, R.S. 1968. Nutrient loss accelerated by clear-cutting of a forest ecosystem. Science. 159: 882-884.

Likens, G.E.; Bormann, F.H.; Johnson, N.M.; Fisher, D.W.; Pierce, R.S. 1970. Effects of forest cutting and herbicide treatment on nutrient budgets in the Hubbard Brook watershed-ecosystem. Ecological Monographs. 40: 23-47.

Pardo, L.H.; Driscoll, C.T.; Likens, G.E. 1995. Patterns of nitrate loss from a chronosequence of clear-cut watersheds. Water, Air, and Soil Pollution. 85: 1659-1664.

Whole-tree harvest effects on soil exchangeable calcium

Clearcutting northern hardwood forests typically causes enhanced export of mineral nutrients, such as calcium, in drainage waters. When these drainage losses are added to the amount of nutrients removed in timber, the total amount of nutrients removed from the ecosystem can be substantial. Thus, changes in soil chemical properties after logging are important in determining the long-term implications of logging on nutrient availability and site fertility. During the winter of 1983-84, W5 was logged by removing whole trees greater than 5 cm d.b.h. Soil exchangeable calcium was measured in mineral and organic soil before (1983) and after (1986, 1991, 1998) the whole-tree harvest. Long-term data from this study indicate that the whole-tree harvest had little effect on the total pool of exchangeable calcium. In the 15 years since the forest was harvested, the cut did not result in the depletion of exchangeable calcium pools, even though a considerable amount of calcium was removed from the ecosystem via increased stream water export and biomass. Soil is the principal source of calcium in these forests, and whole-tree harvesting does not appear to have much of an influence on this nutrient reserve. While there is some evidence of soil calcium depletion in adjacent uncut watersheds, possibly caused by acidic atmospheric deposition, the effects are not evident in the soil exchangeable pool of the aggrading forest at W5.

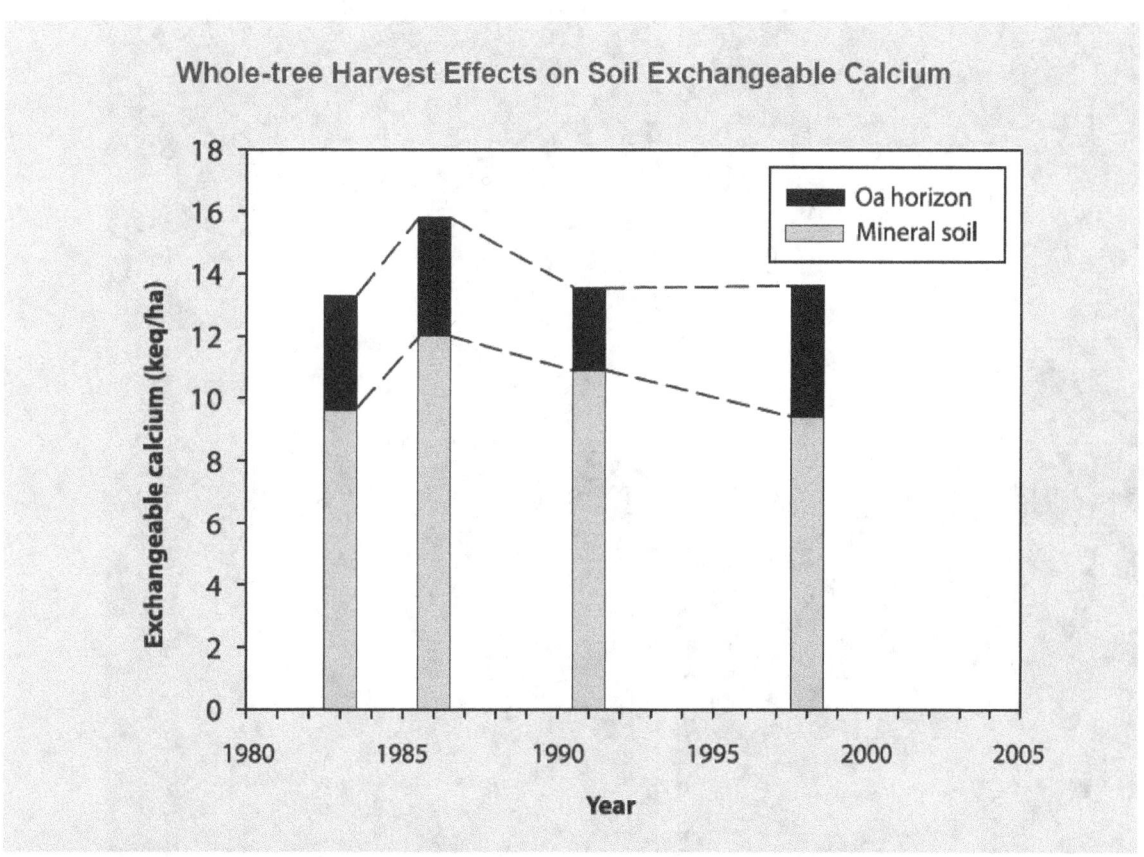

Figure 16. Whole-tree harvest effects on soil exchangeable calcium at W5.

Principal Investigator:

Chris E. Johnson, Syracuse University

Thomas G. Siccama, Yale University

Associated Databases:

Quantitative pit soil carbon and nitrogen (W5), Continuous revegetation survey data (W5)

Further Reading:

Johnson, C.E.; A.H. Johnson, A.H.; Siccama, T.G. 1991. **Whole-tree clear-cutting effects on exchangeable cations and soil acidity.** Soil Science Society of America Journal. 55: 502-508.

Johnson, C.E.; Romanowicz, R.B.; Siccama, T.G. 1997. **Conservation of exchangeable cations after clear-cutting of a northern hardwood forest.** Canadian Journal of Forest Research. 27: 859-868.

Likens, G.E.; Driscoll, C.T.; Buso, D.C.; Siccama, T.G.; Johnson, C.E.; Lovett, G.M.; Fahey, T.J.; Reiners, W.A.; Ryan, D.F.; Martin, C.W.; Bailey, S.W. 1998.
The biogeochemistry of calcium at Hubbard Brook. Biogeochemistry. 41: 89-173.

 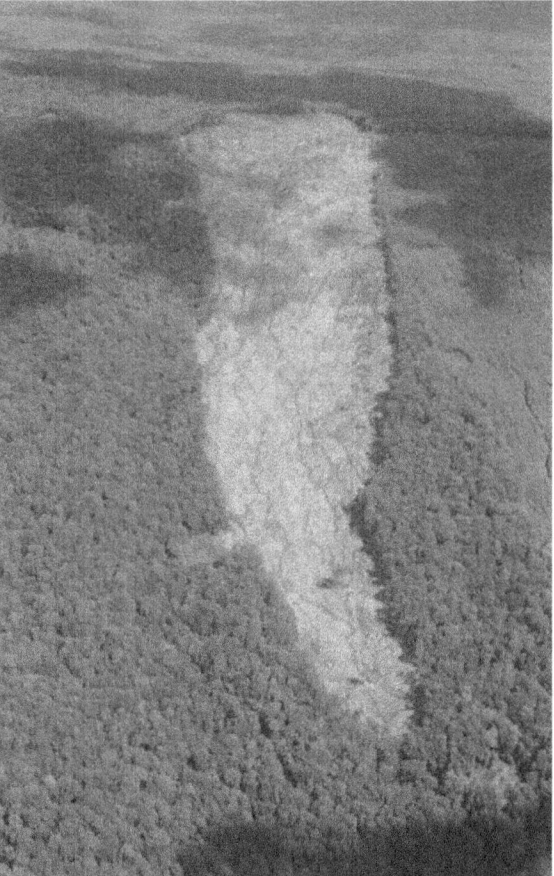

Whole-tree harvest at W5. Photographs: U.S. Forest Service Archives

Calcium concentration in wood fern fronds

Wood fern (*Dryopteris spinulosa*) is the most abundant herbaceous species at the HBEF comprising nearly half of the biomass of that stratum of vegetation. Annual wood fern sampling began in 1985 using consistent methods in an area west of the weir at W6. Each July, fronds are collected and analyzed for several elements including calcium. In the early 1990s, there was a decline in the calcium concentration of wood fern fronds. This pattern is consistent with the idea that calcium is being depleted from soils at the HBEF due to base cation leaching associated with acidic deposition. An experiment was conducted in W1 designed to replace this lost calcium. Pelletized wollastonite ($CaSiO_3$) was added to the entire watershed by aerial application during the fall of 1999. Wood fern was among the first species of vegetation to show a calcium response, with frond concentrations increasing immediately following the wollastonite addition. Despite the general patterns described here, there are several unexplained values, such as the extremely high concentrations at W6 in 2000 and 2004. Further monitoring will help determine what causes these anomalies in the long-term record.

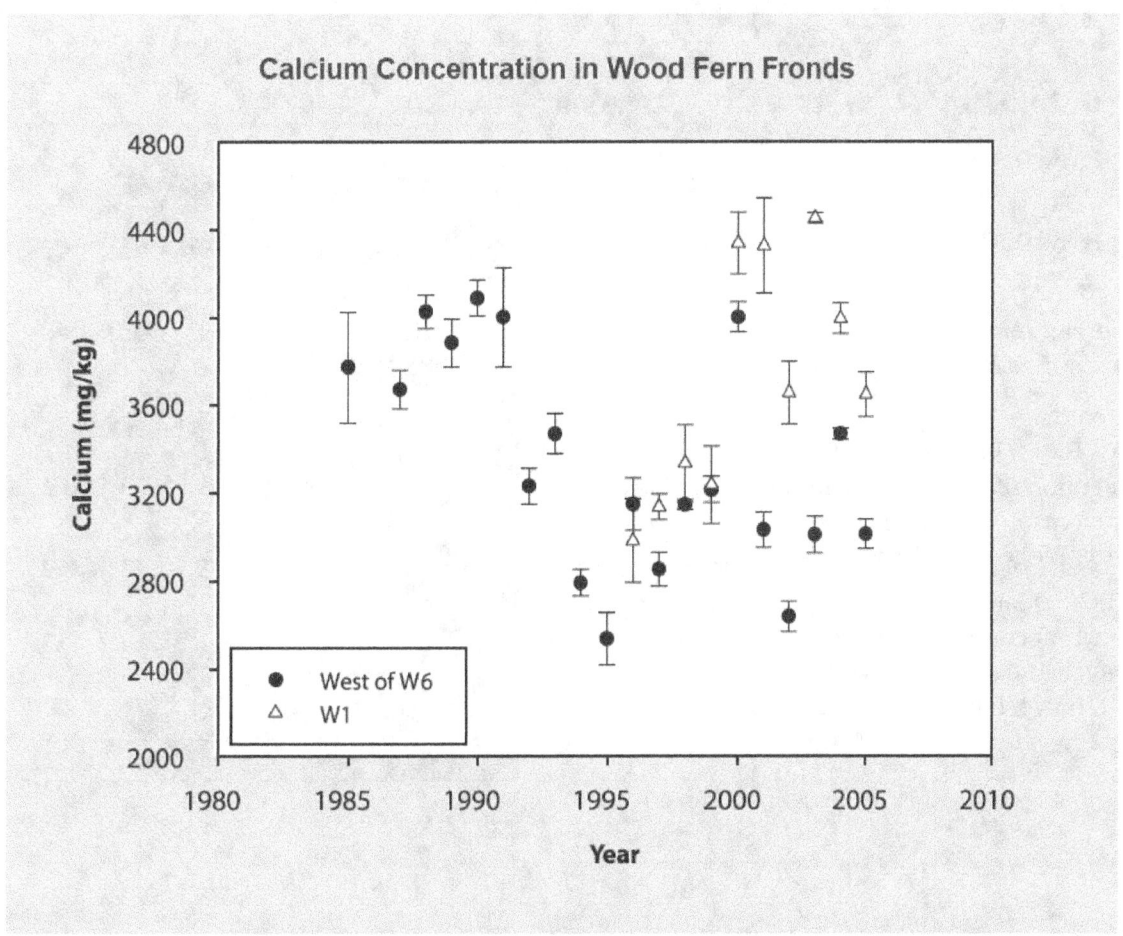

Figure 17. Calcium concentrations (±SE) in wood fern fronds at W1 and west of W6.

Wood ferns (*Dryopteris spinulosa*)

Principal Investigator:

Thomas G. Siccama, Yale University

Associated Databases:

Temporal canopy leaf chemistry (W1 and W6)

Further Reading:

Peters, S.C.; Blum, J.D.; Driscoll, C.T.; Likens, G.E. 2004. **Dissolution of wollastonite during the experimental manipulation of Hubbard Brook Watershed 1.** Biogeochemistry. 67: 309-329.

Siccama, T.G.; Denny, E. 2006. **Long-term changes in the calcium concentration of wood fern fronds** [Online]. Available at http://www.hubbardbrook.org/yale/misc/ferncycl.htm (accessed 29 Sept. 2006).

Aboveground biomass

Aboveground biomass has been measured at plots on two of the experimentally harvested watersheds (W2 and W5) to examine regrowth following disturbance. Watershed 2 was deforested in 1965 followed by 3 successive summers of herbicide treatment. Vegetation was allowed to begin regrowing in 1969 and biomass was measured in years 1, 2, 3, 5, 11, 20 and 31 of regrowth. Watershed 5 underwent a whole-tree harvest in 1984–1985 and aboveground biomass was measured in years 2, 3, 5, 7, 11, 16 and 21 of regrowth. The fast-growing pioneer species, pin cherry, dominates the vegetation on cutover sites at the HBEF and results in particularly high rates of biomass accumulation. For example, in the first 5 years of regrowth, the rate of biomass accumulation on W5 significantly exceeded that on nearby W2, where the abundance of pin cherry was reduced by repeated treatment with herbicides. Reduction in vegetative sprouting and decline in site fertility due to high nutrient leaching probably also contributed to the difference in biomass accumulation between W2 and W5. These differences in vegetation and soils associated with the different treatments appear to have long-lasting effects. During the second decade after disturbance, rates of biomass accumulation accelerated on W5 compared to W2. After 21 years of regrowth, more biomass accumulated on W5 than the amount accumulated after 31 years on W2. Figure adapted from Fahey et al. (2005).

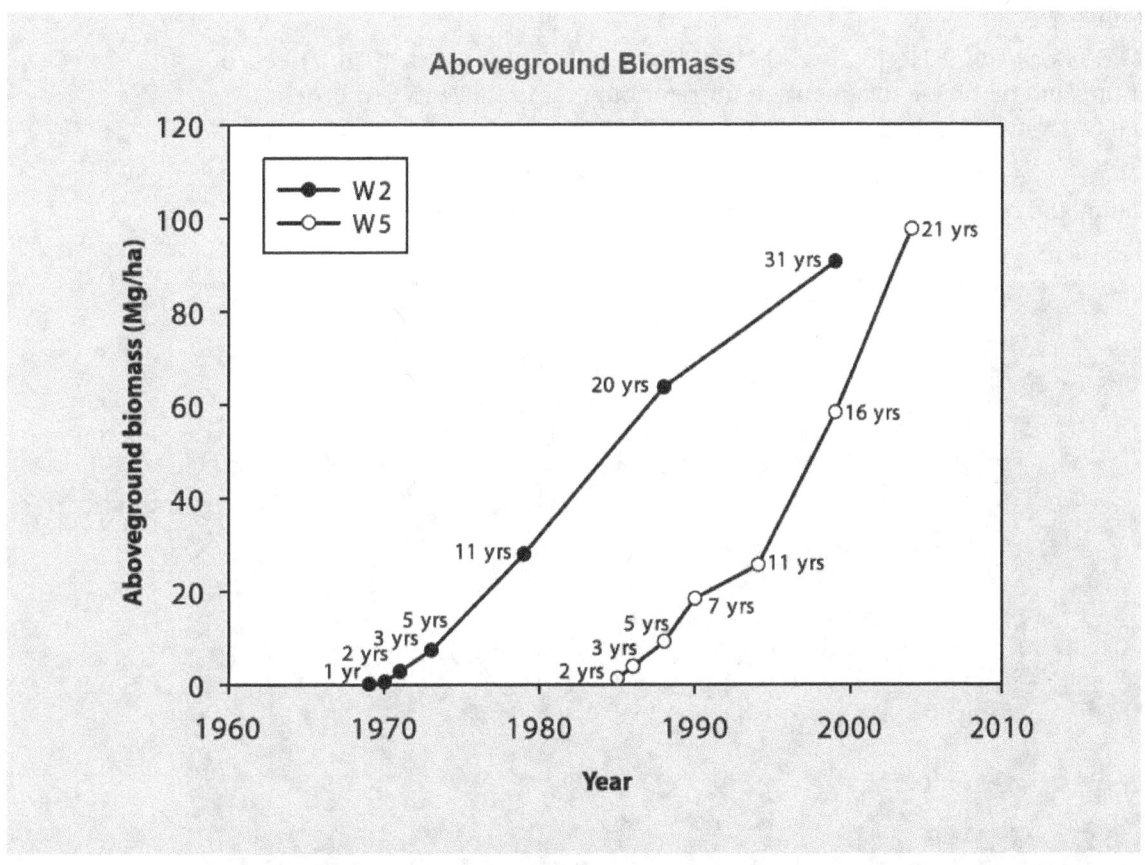

Figure 18. Aboveground biomass at W2 and W5.

Principal Investigators:
Timothy J. Fahey, Cornell University
William A. Reiners, University of Wyoming
Thomas G. Siccama, Yale University

Online Access:
Vegetation recovery (W2) - http://www.hubbardbrook.org/data/dataset.php?id=52
1982 forest inventory (W5) - http://www.hubbardbrook.org/data/dataset.php?id=36
1990 forest inventory (W5) - http://www.hubbardbrook.org/data/dataset.php?id=37
1994 forest inventory (W5) - http://www.hubbardbrook.org/data/dataset.php?id=38
1999 forest inventory (W5) - http://www.hubbardbrook.org/data/dataset.php?id=39

Associated Databases:
Forest inventory (W1, W6, and Bird Transect Area)

Further Reading:

Fahey, T.J.; Siccama, T.G.; Driscoll, C.T.; Likens, G.E.; Campbell, J.; Johnson, C.E.; Battles, J.J.; Aber, J.D.; Cole, J.J.; Fisk, M.C.; Groffman, P.M.; Hamburg, S.P.; Holmes, R.T.; Schwarz, P.A. Yanai, R.D. 2005. **The biogeochemistry of carbon at Hubbard Brook.** Biogeochemistry. 75: 109-176.

Johnson C.E.; Driscoll C.T.; Fahey T.J.; Siccama T.G.; Hughes J.W. 1995. **Carbon dynamics following clearcutting of a northern hardwood forest.** In: McFee W.W.; Kelly J.M. (eds), Carbon forms and functions in forest soils. Madison, WI: American Society of Agronomy: 463-488.

Likens, G.E.; Bormann, F.H.; Johnson, N.M.; Fisher, D.W.; Pierce, R.S. 1970. **Effects of forest cutting and herbicide treatment on nutrient budgets in the Hubbard Brook watershed-ecosystem.** Ecological Monographs. 40: 23-47.

Reiners W.A. 1992. **Twenty years of ecosystem reorganization following experimental deforestation and regrowth suppression.** Ecological Monographs. 62: 503-523.

Aggrading forest stand at the HBEF. Photograph: Nicholas Rodenhouse

Changes in water yield after forest cutting

Experiments were carried out on three of the gaged watersheds to examine the effect of forest cutting on water yield. Experiments included clear-felling and 3 successive years of herbicide applications (W2), strip-cutting (W4), and whole-tree harvesting (W5). Responses in annual water yield varied among treatments, but increased initially and then decreased as the forest regenerated. The increase in water yield following the treatments was short-lived, with the greatest losses occurring at W2 where vegetation regrowth was suppressed by the application of herbicides. Unexpected decreases in annual water yields were evident after the clearfelling and herbicide treatment and after the strip-cutting treatment. These decreases in water yield occurred because newly developing stands dominated by pin cherry and birches have the capacity to transpire more than mature forests, leaving less water available for streamflow. Interestingly, no sustained decreases in water yield occurred on W5 following the whole-tree harvest. Several possible explanations for the different

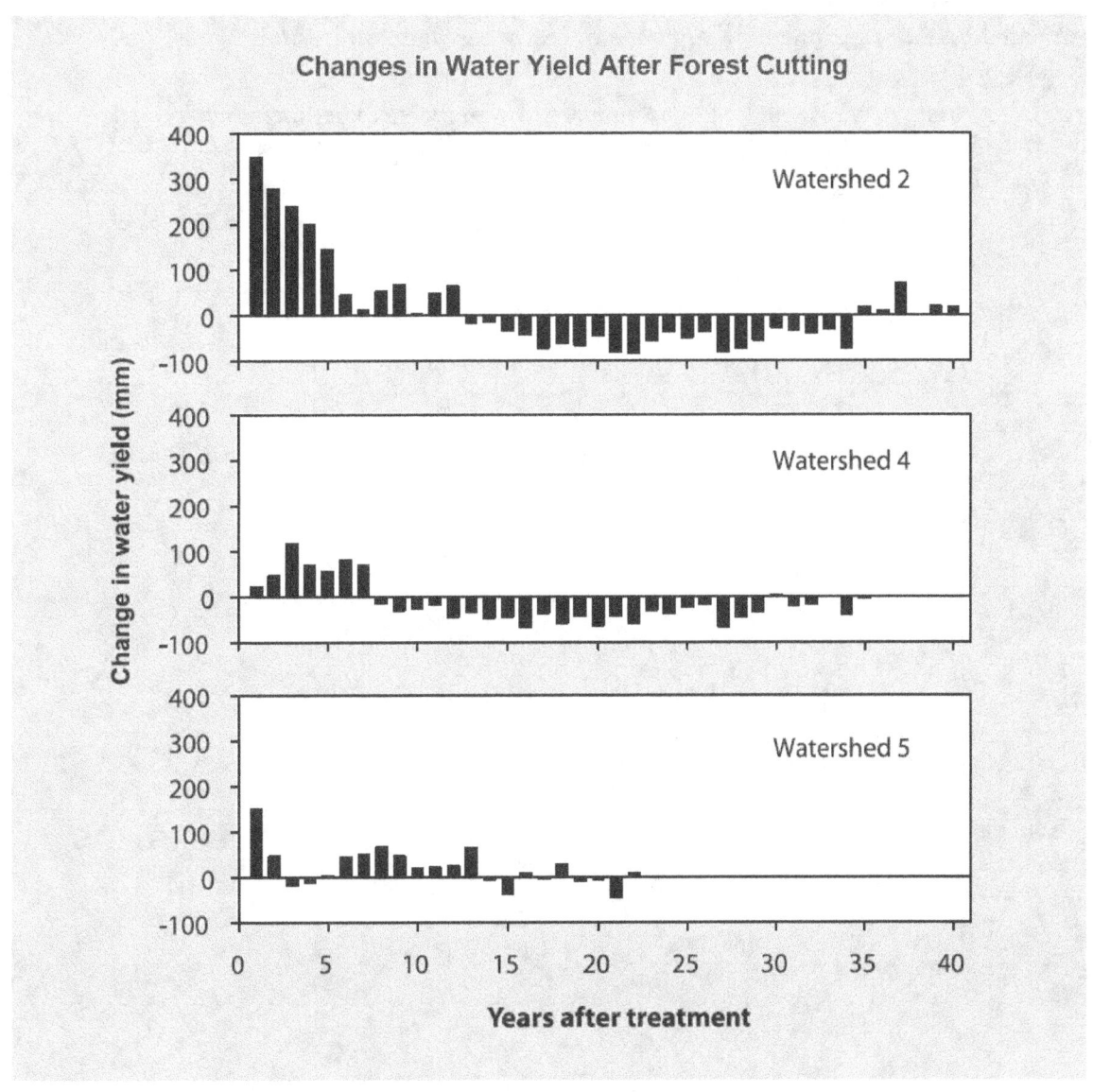

Figure 19. Changes in water yield after forest cutting at W2, W4, and W5.

response at W5 include a lack of regeneration on skid roads, heavy moose browse near the top of the watershed, and a greater proportion of American beech in the regenerating forest. All these factors could reduce transpiration rates without decreasing water yield.

Principal Investigators:
John L. Campbell, U.S. Forest Service
Amey S. Bailey, U.S. Forest Service
Christopher Eagar, U.S. Forest Service

Online Access:
Daily streamflow by watershed - http://www.hubbardbrook.org/data/dataset.php?id=2

Associated Database:
Instantaneous streamflow

Further Reading:
Bailey, A.S.; Hornbeck, J.W.; Campbell, J.L.; Eagar, C. 2003. **Hydrometeorological database for Hubbard Brook Experimental Forest: 1955-2000**. Gen. Tech. Rep. NE-305. Newton Square, PA: U.S. Department of Agriculture, Forest Service, Northeastern Research Station. 36 p.

Hornbeck, J.W.; Martin, C.W.; Eagar, C. 1997. **Summary of water yield experiments at Hubbard Brook Experimental Forest, New Hampshire**. Canadian Journal of Forest Research. 27: 2043-2052.

The use of trade, firm, or corporation names in this publication is for the information and convenience of the reader. Such use does not constitute an official endorsement or approval by the U.S. Department of Agriculture or the Forest Service of any product or service to the exclusion of others that may be suitable.

This publication/database reports research involving pesticides. It does not contain recommendations for their use, nor does it imply that the uses discussed here have been registered. All uses of pesticides must be registered by appropriate State and/or Federal, agencies before they can be recommended.

CAUTION: Pesticides can be injurious to humans, domestic animals, desirable plants, and fish or other wildlife—if they are not handled or applied properly. Use all pesticides selectively and carefully. Follow recommended practices for the disposal of surplus pesticides and pesticide containers.

Campbell, John L.; Driscoll, Charles T.; Eagar, Christopher; Likens, Gene E.; Siccama, Thomas G.; Johnson, Chris E.; Fahey, Timothy J.; Hamburg, Steven P.; Holmes, Richard T.; Bailey, Amey S.; Buso, Donald C. 2007. **Long-term trends from ecosystem research at the Hubbard Brook Experimental Forest.** Gen. Tech. Rep. NRS-17. Newtown Square, PA: U.S. Department of Agriculture, Forest Service, Northern Research Station. 41 p.

Summarizes 52 years of collaborative, long-term research conducted at the Hubbard Brook (NH) Experimental Forest on ecosystem response to disturbances such as air pollution, climate change, forest disturbance, and forest management practices. Also provides explanations of some of the trends and lists references from scientific literature for further reading.

KEY WORDS: biogeochemistry, disturbance, ecosystem, forestry, lake, soil, stream, trends, watershed.

www.ingramcontent.com/pod-product-compliance
Lightning Source LLC
Chambersburg PA
CBHW080622290526
45790CB00007B/2888